CONTENTS

CONTENTS

The Day They Sank

The

LUSITANIA

Chapter 1

THEY'RE OFF!

A SAILING is always exciting, and the bigger the ship the greater the excitement. No train or plane departure, however elaborate, however significant, could pack as big a thrill.

The *Lusitania,* when she departed from New York on Saturday, May 1, 1915, on what was to prove her last voyage, was one of the largest vessels afloat and surely the most popular. Three times she had broken the trans-Atlantic record, which previously had been held by German liners; and, though recently this honor had been taken by her younger sister, *Mauritania,* the "Big Lucy," as her crewmen called her, remained a paragon of speed. Indeed, she was even then being advertised by the Cunard people as the fastest vessel in regular traveler service, for the *Mauritania* had been taken over by the British Admiralty as a troop transport. The Lucy could do 25 knots with ease, and once, five years before, she had *averaged* 26⅓ knots over a 24 hour period, another record.

At Pier 54, at the foot of West 11th Street, it was a morning of drizzling rain to which nobody paid attention.

Another Cunarder, the *Cameronia,* even more recently—in fact, only a few hours ago—had been seized by the British Admiralty. Her passengers-to-be, already aboard and suddenly finding themselves without transportation, were offered equivalent accommodations on the nearby *Lusitania;* and 41 of them, delighted, accepted. This last-minute transfer added to the stir. It also delayed the sailing, scheduled for ten o'clock.

There was another and even bigger reason for all the fuss. The previous day there had appeared in papers throughout the land this paid announcement:

NOTICE

Travelers intending to embark on the Atlantic voyage are reminded that a state of war exists between Germany and her allies, and Great Britain and her allies; and the zone of war includes the waters adjacent to the British Isles; that, in accordance with formal notice given by the Imperial German Government, vessels flying the flag of Great Britain, or any of her allies, are liable to destruction in those waters and that travelers sailing in the

war zone on ships of Great Britain or her allies
do so at their own risk.

Imperial German Embassy
Washington, D.C., April 22, 1915.

It certainly sounded like a threat, though there
were many who laughed at it, including the New
York agent for the line, Charles P. Sumner. He said
that he simply could not believe the German embassy had done such a thing, even though the newspapers assured him the advertisement had come from
a reputable Washington agency. (The ambassador
himself was not to be reached for the weekend, and
nobody else at the embassy would say anything.)
Sumner thought that it was another attempt to
blackmail the Cunard Line; there had been other
threats—bomb threats—before.

"As for submarines," he added, "I have no fear of
them whatsoever."

Theodore Roosevelt, the former President of the
U.S., did not agree. He thought that the notice was
an insult to the American people, and he said as
much, heatedly, in Syracuse.

Why Syracuse? Because an upstate Republican
boss, William Barnes, Jr., who resented being called
a crook by the outspoken Rough Rider, was suing
for libel; and the trial was being held in Syracuse.
This trial promised to prove a three-ring circus, as
anything in which Teddy of the Big Stick played a
part was sure to be. The public was vastly amused.
You could say what you wanted about this man

Wilson, but he never put on the show that Teddy did.

"I'm going to nail Roosevelt's hide to the fence," the chief Barnes lawyer, William M. Ivins, had boasted to Elihu Root.

"Look, Ivins, let me give you a piece of advice," Root had responded. "I know Roosevelt, and you want to be very sure that it's *his* hide you get on that fence."

He was right. Once the Colonel took the witness stand there was no holding him. He made speeches in all directions, and they were bright speeches, too. The public was fascinated. To a great many Americans on that Saturday morning, the Roosevelt-Barnes trial in Syracuse was at least as interesting a story, and a darned sight funnier, than the war in Europe. The papers were full of it. Men on the streets talked about little else.

Aboard the Big Lucy reporters understandably solicited the distinguished passengers for their opinion of the notice. To a man, the questionees tut-tutted.

"In my opinion it was a very silly performance of the German Embassy," said Charles T. Bowring of Bowring Brothers, shipowners.

Sir Hugh Lane, the art collector, thought it "too absurd for discussion."

Cablegrams revealed that the principal Liverpool shippers—the *Lusitania* was headed for Liverpool—were calling it "another piece of German bluff," and this was the general opinion at the foot of West 11th Street that eventful Saturday morning.

"I think it is a lot of tommyrot for any government to do such a thing, and it is hard to believe that the German ambassador dictated the advertisement," declared Alexander Campbell, general manager of John Dewar and Sons, London. "The *Lusitania* can run away from any submarine the Germans have got, and the British Admiralty will see she is looked after when she arrives in striking distance of the Irish coast."

This being settled, the visitors were shooed ashore. It was 12:30. There was a terrific blast of the ship's whistle. Stewards scurried; passengers waved; and the band, unheard, played doggedly on. Three tugs, actually big ones but looking tiny by the side of this giantess of the sea, fussed her out to midstream. Smoke was pouring from her four great red-and-black stacks. The drizzle had ceased, the skies were clear again, and sunlight gilded the vessel as she started for the bay, the Narrows, and the Atlantic.

She had been a familiar sight in New York ever since her launching eight years back, but she still thrilled those who watched her. Now thousands, turning aside from their ordinary work on tugs and ferries and other harbor craft, on docks, and at the windows of skyscrapers, watched her as she went. Everybody loved the Lucy.

Chapter 2

GOODBY, MADHOUSE

IT WAS A CRAZY SORT of city they sailed away from. It was a hive of fads, humming with bizarre notions. Its favorite movie was *The Birth of a Nation*, its favorite preacher Bill Sunday, an ex-baseball player, and the militant suffragettes with their slogan, "Votes for Women," were its favorite target for mockery. It was wont to laugh as well, especially on Sundays, at the antics of Happy Hooligan, the Katzenjammer Kids, Buster Brown and his dog Tige, Mutt and Jeff, Alphonse and Gaston, and the hall room boys, Percy and Ferdy.

The war seemed far away, something that those Europeans, who were always fighting anyway, had stirred up by themselves—and they could damn well keep it.

Macy's was charging 69¢ for a full quart of real Spanish olive oil. Arnold, Constable and Co. had women's lisle silk stockings at 25¢ a pair. Gimbel's was currently featuring the matching frock and parasol; but *all* the stores carried the latest craze in women's footwear, above-the-ankle boots that laced down the side. Lord and Taylor's, taking advantage of the fashion, and of the shortage it had created, had these in "Putty and Gray Glacé Kid," and were asking $5.50 a pair. Still, a mode is a mode, and a lady couldn't afford to be behind the times, now could she?

As for the men, they were sporting buck-tops, and some, the classier, even Oxford ties. Gimbel's was advertising men's suits at $15—"$20 and $25 suits have nothing on these"—but Altman's charged $17.50, Brokaw Brothers $18, and Stern's, the scoundrels, $18.50.

The game of auction bridge—some preferred the more high-toned name of Bath Club bridge—was, if not actually sweeping the country, then at least causing a great many heads to be scratched, and brows to be knitted. Old-timers snorted that bridge-whist would never be supplanted, but there was no doubt that the new game was catching on. It was complicated. Instead of the dealer or the dealer's partner making a simple declaration as to trumps, there was competitive bidding, and the one who bid the highest played the hand. The scoring, too, was totally different. Still and all, the game was fashionable, and it might well be here to stay.

Traffic always had been bad in New York but, lately, in addition to the usual drays, pushcarts, trolley cars, hansom cabs, horse omnibuses, and the elegant turn-outs of the Fifth Avenue set, there was a horde of noisy, malodorous automobiles. You saw and heard and smelled them on every avenue and often enough on the crosstown streets as well. They multiplied like ants, and so the price went down. No longer were they rich men's hobbies. An Overland 6 would set you back $1,475 FOB Toledo; a Paige, $1,395; and a Cole 8, $1,785. But you could get a Maxwell ("Every Road's a Maxwell Road") for $695; a Ford for $490. That last bargain was even better than it sounded. The master of Dearborn, always interested in sharing profits with his customers, had decreed that if more than 300,000 Model T's were sold between August 1, 1914 and August 1, 1915 each buyer would get a rebate. The sale came to 308,213, and so 308,213 checks of $50 each were mailed out.

If not utterly everybody was doing the Turkey Trot, at least a great many were. The One Step and the Bunnie Hug too, but chiefly the Turkey Trot. They were inspired to this in part because of the Victor Company advertisement that showed— together with a talking machine, handle and all— that endearing young couple, Vernon and Irene Castle. It was easy to dance, readers were assured. You could teach yourself, with the aid of the machine.

Victor, however, was aware that Tin Pan Alley was not all; for the American people, those in New York especially, had an aesthetic streak, and only the other day Geraldine Farrar and Maria Barrientos had consented to new Metropolitan Opera contracts for the 1915-16 season. Victor had signed them exclusively as recording artists, together with Caruso, Scotti, Martinelli, Schumann-Heinck, Frieda Hemple, and many others, leaving the young firm of Columbia with little in the way of stars left. Columbia was not to be out-cultured, however. In the papers the very day the *Lusitania* sailed, Columbia came out with large announcements of "the first opera ever completely recorded." This was *Aïda,* and the job had been done in Milan, Italy. The singers were unnamed, but the implication was that they were good, at least as good as Caruso, et al. There were seventeen records, which sold for 75¢ each.

True, visitors to New York not infrequently were put through a wringer at the cabarets; but this was their lookout. For example, Reisenweber's in Columbus Circle unblushingly charged $1 for its table d'hote, and the waiters expected and sometimes received a ten percent tip, though at least there was no extra charge for the floor show, *Too Much Mustard.* Churchill's ("More than a Restaurant, a Broadway Institution") and its principal rival, Shanley's, put on twenty acts every night, and they had the nerve to ask $1.25 for the dinner; lunch was 75¢. But these were tourist traps. By just asking around a bit a man could find meals that were much more reasonable.

That very afternoon the Yankees defeated Connie Mack's Athletics to get into first place in the American League, the Athletics dropping to second. This was at the Polo Grounds. Meanwhile, in Philadelphia the Phillies were trouncing the National League

New York Giants, even though Christy Mathewson himself, with his famous "fadeaway," was on the mound.

More than of the doings of baseball players, New Yorkers were enamored of the doings of the Idle Rich, High Society, the Four Hundred, who, for their part, did nothing to dodge the limelight. Quiet good taste was out of fashion. Whoopla reigned supreme; and the public loved it.

Only last night, for instance, that intrepid African big-game hunter Lady Grace Mackenzie had given a "jungle dinner" for a few select friends at Delmonico's. The guests included two lion cubs, two cheetahs, one leopard cub, and one black ape. Potted palms were everywhere, giving a tropical effect. The cats were on leashes five or six feet long and on platforms around the walls, from where they snarled most realistically. The ape was at large. The enormous table had a lion's skin for a centerpiece; there were bronze statues of rhinoceros and buffalo at either end. Jungle fruits were "strewn about sporadically," and the menu featured such tasty items as stuffed eagles' eggs, rhinoceros tongues, cucumber Kikiyu and Egyptian quail. The party was a huge success. Of course Theodore Roosevelt, that "combination of St. Paul and St. Vitus," the man who "killed lions as though they were mosquitoes and mosquitoes as though they were lions," had been invited. He responded with a telegram of regret, from Syracuse.

In ordinary circumstances there would have been more than a sprinkling of these Idle Rich aboard the

Lusitania, for she was popular with the exalted; but the war, after all, meant *something,* and a surprisingly large number of the passengers in every class was doctors or nurses who meant to offer their services to the British Red Cross. Another surprisingly large number were children, 129 of them, mostly in second class. There were 290 passengers in first class, 600 in second class, and 367 in third.

Easily the most resplendent, the most illustrious of what representatives of High Society there were aboard the *Lusitania* was Alfred Gwynne Vanderbilt, a slim, tall, dark, strikingly handsome man of 37, tweedy, quiet, with a fondness for ascot ties and cockily canted caps. Nobody knew just how much he was worth—probably he did not know himself—but it was certainly upward of $60,000,000. He was a great-grandson of Commodore Cornelius Vanderbilt, the founder of the fortune, and though he was a younger son he had inherited the bulk of the estate left by his father, Cornelius Vanderbilt II. The older son, Cornelius III, had been cut off with a mere $1,500,000, since Cornelius II had not approved of his marriage. Alfred Gwynne, however, had helped to assuage his older brother's grief by a voluntary gift of $5,000,000, just so that Cornelius III could live in the style to which it can be assumed he was accustomed.

A Yale man, Alfred G. Vanderbilt went in for polo, automobile racing and, most of all, four-in-hand driving, which fascinated him. He owned 48 shares of Metropolitan Horse Shows, Ltd., of London, and 415 shares of National Horse Shows of

America, and he was aboard the *Lusitania* because he planned to attend a meeting of the directors of the International Horse Show Association in London.

Since he was a celebrity, he had of course been cornered by reporters at pierside.

Though he habitually favored the *Lusitania,* three years before, on a whim, he had booked westbound passage on the *Titanic* when she was about to make her maiden—and only—voyage. On another whim he had cancelled this reservation at the last moment. Now a reporter asked him about this. Did he believe that he led a charmed life? Vanderbilt smiled mysteriously, but made no comment.

He spoke up, however, when they asked him if he wasn't afraid of submarine attack. He shrugged.

"Why? We can outdistance any submarine afloat."

He occupied a cabin on A Deck, on the starboard side, a cabin he did not often leave. He had most of his meals brought there by his valet, Roland Denyer. This was not because he held himself above the common herd, but because he did not enjoy being pointed out. He was sick of the so-called Social Swim. He would not have been amused by Lady Mackenzie's "jungle dinner" last night.

Chapter 3

SIX COLD BOILERS

THE FIRST 24 HOURS they made 501 miles. This would have been fast for any other vessel: for the Big Lucy it was just poking along. Moreover, it was to prove the best run of the crossing, for thereafter the figure fell down to the 460's.

Off the coast of Nova Scotia early on Sunday, the first full day out, they did encounter patches of fog; but these were soon passed and the weather the rest of the way across was to be perfect. Why, then, didn't they go faster?

This question was often asked, and by none more earnestly than Charles E. Lauriat, Jr., member of a Boston firm of booksellers, who was traveling on business. It was by no means young Lauriat's first crossing—it was, in fact, his twenty-third, for his company maintained a London office—but it was the first time he had taken a fast ship; and he was disappointed. Time after time he picked a high figure in the pool, and time after time he lost. The *Lusitania* continued to dawdle along at 19 or 20 knots.

Lauriat decided that the skipper, a colorful salt named Turner, who had gone to sea in sail at the age of eight, was holding the big boat in reserve for the last final dash along the south coast of Ireland. Once they got within the war zone, he predicted, they'd really show some speed.

Lauriat was a friendly man and he expressed this view many times. On the whole, the others in first class agreed with him. Yes, that must be it. The captain was saving steam for a last-minute sprint.

That was *not* it, as any officer, if pressed, might have told them.

Undeniably the *Lusitania* was fast. She had been built in 1907 by John Brown of Clydebank, Scotland, and she was something brand new, revolutionary, in the history of steamships. In the first place, she was enormous. She was 769 feet from stem to stern, almost one-seventh of a mile (one of the Cunard Line advertisements in New York showed the three principal skyscrapers, the Flatiron, the St. Paul, and the Park Row buildings, piled one on top of the other next to an upended *Lusitania;* they were only a trifle longer), and her beam was 88 feet, her depth 60 feet 4 inches, her displacement 41,400 tons. She was heavy: 26,000 steel plates, some of them weighing five tons, were held together by 4,000,000 rivets weighing, in all, 500 tons. Her rudder alone weighed 65 tons, and she carried three anchors each 10 tons in weight.

Many of her luxury features—the electric elevators, for example—were "firsts." So were the wood-burning fireplaces in the lounge. So were the dog kennels, and the playpens.

She had a double bottom five feet deep, separated into 175 watertight compartments that ran both fore-and-aft and abeam. Even later superliners, excepting the *Mauretania,* did not have such underwater protection. If that iceberg had crashed into the *Lusitania* instead of the *Titanic* on the night of April 15, 1912, engineers said at the time, there wouldn't have been a sinking; the Lucy could have made it home.

The most radical departure of all was in her power. She had four huge steam turbines, with 3,000,000 individual blades, which would surely cause her four propellers to send her through the water faster than any other vessel had ever gone.

This prediction came true. The *Lusitania* arrived off Sandy Hook at the end of her maiden voyage on September 13, 1907, having shaved a good six hours from the existing record, held by the North German Lloyd liner *Kaiser Wilhelm II.* Old tars, notoriously a superstitious lot, were to point out, with shaking heads and clucking tongues, that that particular September 13 was a Friday, which boded no good for the Lucy. Her career had refuted this. She had twice broken her own speed record, in 1908 and 1909, and she was surely one of the most popular ships afloat. She always had a waiting list.

All this had been in the piping times of peace. War made everything different.

For such a mammoth to make money she would have to sail full, or virtually full, hold and cabins alike, on every crossing. This was easy enough at first. Even in wartime there would be plenty of cargo both ways. She was presently carrying 50,000 tons of sheet brass, 32,000 tons of copper and copper wire, 21,000 tons of copper manufactures, 31,000 tons of beef, 119,000 tons of furs, 4,200 cases of cartridges for small arms, and 1,250 empty steel shrapnel shells—a total of 1,500 tons of cargo. This was valued at about $750,000. The ship itself had cost $6,500,000 to build, but the fittings brought this up to more than $10,000,000, so that ship and cargo together could be said to be worth close to $11,000,-000, a rich prize. It was insured for $7,500,000 at the regular five percent premium, plus an extra war premium of only one and a quarter percent. The war premium was this low because of the *Lusitania*'s speed.

On the other hand, passenger bookings would be sure to fall off, even with the *Mauretania* and now the *Cameronia* taken out of private service. The Cunard men pondered this. The Lucy was too big to be used anywhere else in the world. To put her temporarily out of commission would be much too expensive. Also, there was good will to be remembered; there was reputation, prestige; and the war wasn't going to last forever.

It was finally decided to keep the Lucy on her usual run but to close down six of her 25 boilers.

This would not only save on stokers, it would save on coal as well. On this trip she carried only 6,000 tons of her 7,000-ton coal capacity. But closing down the boilers would cut speed. There would be no more 25-knot runs for the duration. A shade better than 20 was about as much as the Lucy could do now.

Understandably, the company did not shout this bit of news from the housetops. If it was not exactly a secret, at least the passengers were unaware of it.

There were 1,265 of those passengers—almost 300 in first class, twice that number in second class, while third class or steerage, with less than 400, was filled to only about one-third of its capacity. Even so, this was the largest number of passengers any vessel had carried eastbound so far that year. One hundred and eighty-nine of them were Americans.

There was another matter that would have interested the passengers, if they had known of it. This was the fact that the Big Lucy did not have her regular, complete crew.

Again it was the fault of the war. Some of the best officers and deck men had been members of the Royal Naval Reserve or the Fleet Reserve, and as such had been called to the colors. These had, of course, been replaced; but some of the new hands were raw, and in any event a ship's crew, like a football team or a symphony orchestra, must be something much more than the sum of its individual abilities. The skipper, William Turner, at 63 had commanded some of the finest vessels afloat; and the chief engineer, Archibald Bryce (a man with overpowering walrus mustaches) was also one of the best in the business, having worked for the Cunard Line for more than 30 years. Still, there were bound to be weak spots. The officers and men had been working together for only a few months. These things can count.

The *Lusitania* did not sail shorthanded, however, There were 77 men in the deck department, 314 in the engineering department (fewer than usual because of the closed-down boilers, but enough), 306 in the stewards' department and five musicians. This made 702 in all, 677 of them male, 25 female.

The *Lusitania* was listed by Lloyd's as 100 A-1.

Chapter 4

IN LOW ESTEEM

ONE THING decidedly was not a secret, and that was the possibility of a submarine attack. The passengers in each class, and members of the crew as well, talked of little else.

Few if any were afraid, but the chance of a chase made a spicy topic of conversation, once the deck chairs had been set out and the tea and bouillon served. It was an excellent way to get acquainted. Everybody had an opinion.

All, though, were agreed on one thing: that they were lucky to be aboard the Big Lucy. Not only had there been no cancellations, but unexpected passengers, such as the transferees from the *Cameronia,* and Madame Maria de Page, wife of Dr. Antoine de Page, director of the La Panne Hospital in Belgium, considered themselves singularly blessed. Madame de Page had been in the United States in order to raise funds for the Belgian Red Cross. She had intended to take an earlier, slower ship home, but had postponed her departure to make a few more speaking engagements and raise a little more money. Now she was delighted to find herself aboard the *Lusitania*.

All of this optimism was founded on two rather simple assumptions: first, that even when she was creeping along like this at a mere 20 knots, the Big Lucy could easily outpace any submarine in the world; and second, that if she were hit she wouldn't sink anyway.

People did not know much about submarines and their torpedoes, the building and operation of which were shrouded in secrecy. The speed argument was always advanced as unanswerable, it being the popular belief that a submarine commander would permit possible prey to pass him and then would give chase. Even so knowledgeable a mariner as Captain Turner did not propose to zigzag when he reached the war zone, for it was his understanding that you only zigzagged *after* you had been attacked, presumably in order to avoid catching a torpedo in the tail.

Nor did it occur to anybody to point out that while a 12-knot submarine would be a rarity, a 40-knot Whitehead torpedo (the compressed air type, named after its English inventor) would not. Or that a sub skipper might find it advisable to intercept an enemy vessel rather pursue it.

The truth is, most civilians and even many high-ranking Navy men were disinclined to take the submarine seriously. It was most interesting, a most promising invention; but of course it was still in the experimental stage. Inventors, as everyone knew, were long-haired fanatics, not normal people like you and me. They lived in a world of their own, a suburb of Never-Never Land. *They* did not have to do the fighting. *Theirs* was not the ultimate responsibility of the battlefield. There were assuredly great possibilities in the submarine as a weapon, and these might in time be developed, but in the navies of the world—and this included the Imperial German Navy—it was pointed out again and again that the sub had no speed and no fire power worth mentioning. How, then, could it be expected to measure up to conventional war vessels? How, even, could it be expected to hang up much of a record as a destroyer of large vessels? Sure, it might make a stir in terror-spreading, hit-and-run operations against small craft, fishing vessels and the like, but that, at the present stage, was about the sum of its usefulness.

After all, there was something unmilitary, something a bit *sneaky,* about shooting at men who can't see you, and who are expecting no trouble. As the British would say, it wasn't cricket.

Submarines at that time, like planes, did not constitute an elite service. The men who handled them were admired perhaps for their courage, but at the same time they were pitied for their attachment to an unstable, dangerous, expensive, and at best unpredictable and almost useless contraption. You needed more than courage to be a good soldier, a good sailor. You needed more than dedication. You needed a sense of reality—something airplane pilots and submariners did not have.

A sub might mount a three- or four-inch deck gun, but any Coast Guard cutter could send such a craft to the bottom in ten seconds flat. The submarine's primary weapon was the torpedo; and the amount of ignorance concerning the Whitehead torpedo, even among naval officers and engineers, was colossal. Since its invention it had been vastly improved, but an intensive hush-hush had sheathed these improvements, and indeed changes in the construction and operation of Whitehead torpedoes for years had been one of the chief interests of international spies. The average nonsubmarine Navy officer might have seen a new Whitehead now and then, and he might even have watched them being launched, if he happened to be assigned to destroyers; but the deck-launched, surface-skimming torpedoes were never as accurate as those fired from a submerged submarine. The nonsubmarine officer did not know this—and of course the civilian didn't.

The very nickname the gobs assigned to torpedoes, the derisive "tin fish," tended to lower the weapon in their own estimation as well as in that of the public. But the truth was somewhat different. A typical submarine torpedo of 1915 might be 12 or 14 feet long or longer. It might weigh a ton. It could travel at 40 knots for the first 1,000 yards, and its gyroscope and its two compressed air-driven propellers, turning different ways, kept it just underneath the surface, so that it would be a difficult target, its presence being indicated only by a swiftly disappearing strip of bubbles. It was no longer a plaything. It packed a tremendous warhead.

It is possible, too, that Americans may have derided the torpedo because of a memory of learning in school that at the start of the battle of Mobile Bay the Union admiral, Farragut, cried: "Damn the torpedoes, full steam ahead!" But Farragut was not talking about a self-propelled, cigar-shaped, fast, deadly missile, but rather a round, gunpowder-packed, free-floating object that today we would call a mine; but this was not generally known.

The average person, then, still thought of the submarine as a pesky but essentially harmless device. The average person was to learn his mistake.

Chapter 5

ALONE AGAINST THE NAVY

FOR MANY YEARS the design and construction of
submarines had been in Navy hands or at least under Navy orders, the reason being that the work
was much too expensive for any private person,
much too unprofitable for any private company. At
one time the sub had been envisioned as an explor-
ing device and even as a cargo carrier, but it had
come to be realized that it was and would be exclusively a war machine.

It was not always thus. Civilians had started the
submarine.

Alexander the Great was reputed to have gone
down to the bottom of the sea in what might have
been an early diving bell; but then, many stories
were told about Alexander the Great, and will continue to be.

It is certain, however, that the ancient Greeks had

frogmen for naval operations, and they might have had diving bells as well.

Leonardo da Vinci, who thought of everything, thought of building a submarine. He even designed one. But he tore up his plans after he decided that here was too touchy a matter for mankind to meddle with.

The first record of a vessel that actually *proceeded* under water is the nebulous one about the large wooden rowboat that Cornelius van Dreble, a Dutchman residing in England, covered with heavily oiled leather and navigated slightly below the surface of the Thames in 1620. It was propelled by twelve oarsmen. Tradition, nothing else, has it that James I took a ride in this contrivance. It is hard to believe. James I, though a Stuart, was an exceedingly timid man. Nor do any details survive as to how a boat could be rowed under water, or why it should be.

Van Dreble may never have lived, but there is no doubt that David Bushnell did. Bushnell, a Yale graduate living in Saybrook, Connecticut, for years had been fooling with the idea of an underwater boat, and in 1776 he actually built one. He called it the *Turtle.*

It must have looked more like an upended oyster. It was made of oak planks banded together with iron. It was seven feet long, four feet wide, eight feet high—just large enough to hold one man. Bushnell, in a series of tests in the Connecticut River, trained his brother Ezra to operate it.

Whether on the surface or submerged it moved in an upright position, 700 pounds of lead in the bottom keeping it that way. On the floor there was a water tank, and there were two small brass forcing pumps, worked by foot, for bringing in or pushing out liquid ballast. There was no depth meter, but none was needed, for the operator soon learned that at a depth of 18 feet tar began to ooze through the seams. He did not even have to see it, he could smell it. There was a compass.

At the top was a tiny conning tower, just large enough for a man's head, its sides consisting of slabs of glass. There was no periscope. Fully submerged, the driver was blind.

The stem and stern were like the lips of a clam. Forward and outside, moved by means of a hand crank combined with a pedal arrangement, was a small screw propeller, the first in history. Astern, waggled by an inside tiller, was a minute rudder. The craft would go backward or forward, depending upon which way the crank was turned. There was a small screw propeller mounted horizontally on top of the conning tower. This, geared to a separate crank, was for diving or rising.

Previous machines, designed to slam an "infernal" or "water petard" against the side of an enemy vessel, had been hit-and-run contraptions. Bushnell proposed to approach the vessel in silence, coming up beneath the hull. The infernal itself, a waterproof sack of gunpowder rigged with floats to make it buoyant and operated by a clockwork mechanism— possibly the first time that *this* was ever so used— could be detached from the inside of the *Turtle,* whether submerged or on the surface.

Early on a morning in September this apparatus was launched at the foot of the Battery in New York City. Not only was it an historic occasion, it was a damned spooky one as well. The fortunes of the nation that had only just declared its independence were at a low point. The British and Hessians in overwhelming force had taken Staten Island. They had crossed to Long Island and taken it, too, seizing at the same time many prisoners, including two major generals. They could cross to Manhattan Island and take that any day now. Washington was desperate, which no doubt is why he consented to the first submarine attack in history, for his was a conventional military mind and ordinarily he would have shied away from such unorthodox methods.

The Britsh fleet, under Lord Howe, lay at anchor in the upper bay, its flagship, *HMS Eagle,* near Governor's Island. The attack was to be made on the *Eagle,* a 60-gunner. In the unlikely event that she was sunk or badly damaged, all the rest of the powerful fleet would remain, and any unit of this would be enough to blast out of the water anything the Continentals could send against it; but the fear of the unknown, the fear of a sneak attack, might well be spread among the at present power-cocky British tars; and that would help.

The night was dark, no moon, no stars. The air was chilly. A little group of officers, among them Israel Putnam, gathered on the sea wall at the southern tip of Manhattan to watch the launching. Ezra wriggled into the contraption.

It was not Ezra Bushnell, who had been taken ill, but a last-minute substitute, Ezra Lee of Lyme, Connecticut, a sergeant in the Continental Army and a man of steel nerves.

The thing had been carefully planned. Lee was to be helped by the tide on his way out, and after he had done his deed the just-turned tide would help him back. However, unexpected delays put him behind schedule, and he had scarcely got a good start when he felt the tide turning, tugging him back toward shore. He struggled hard, working against time as well as tide, for soon it would be daylight; and at long last, after almost superhuman exertions, he found himself in the very midst of the greatest fleet in the world—he, one man, encased in a cockleshell.

They loomed all around him, those sea giants. He could hear the lazy rattle of chains, the squeal of timbers, the shouts of lookouts to quarterdecks, the tramp of patrolling quartermasters.

If he was spotted, if he was challenged, he was lost. Almost anything, conceivably even a musket ball, could cripple his frail boat, and Ezra Lee, if he wasn't drowned, assuredly would be hanged as a spy.

Already there were streakings of dawn in the east.

He found the *Eagle*. He took one last deep breath, and dove. He came up underneath her.

The most ingenious part of Bushnell's ingenious device now was brought into play. Just above the operator's head, next to the minute conning tower,

was an up-pointing borer, a screw, which likewise
could be worked from the inside of the submarine.
The plan was to drill a niche into the underside of
the vessel and fit the infernal into this, so that it
would not slip away or be carried off by the current.

Sergeant Lee started to turn the borer. Nothing
happened. It wouldn't bite.

Some of the British vessels, those that had lately
been on the West Indies station, had their bottoms
sheathed with copper as protection against the tor-
edo worm. The *Eagle* might have been one of these,
but this possibility, too, had been taken into consid-
eration. The borer was designed to drill right
through copper sheathing. Lee must have encountered something more solid. One of the iron strips
supporting the rudder post?

Working in the dark—the needle and card of his
compass had been smeared with phosphorus, but
this gave only the faintest glow—he shifted to another place, bumping up again. Still the borer would not
take hold.

He was out of air. The clockwork fuse would go
off at any moment. And it must be full daylight by
now. He dived, pedaled a short distance, and surfaced, gasping.

It *was* daylight, and almost immediately he was
seen and challenged. A ship's boat was put overside
and it started toward him. He detached the bomb
and frantically paddled away from it.

The boat could have overtaken him in a matter of
seconds, but the bosun's mate in charge of it was

leery of that floating sack. He paused to give it a good look. And the thing went off.

It caused a terrific explosion and sent a column of water mast high into the air. Nobody was hurt and nothing was damaged, but the blast threw a serious scare into the breasts of thousands of British tars, and in the ensuing confusion Ezra Lee of Lyme, that brave man, made the shore unhurt.

Chapter 6

O, PIONEERS!

BUSHNELL AT LEAST had proved that gunpowder could be exploded under water. After one more abortive attempt he put the *Turtle* aside, releasing Sergeant Lee to routine duties, and experimented with an infernal mounted in a whaleboat, which he drove against the British frigate *Cerberus* off New London, Connecticut, August 15, 1777. It fell short, and was seen and hauled up on deck by four sailors, who started to take the cover off. One of those sailors was knocked overboard. He was lucky; he lived. The other three were blown to pieces.

This would come under the head not of submarines but of torpedoes, as would the next experiment of David Bushnell who, in January 1778, another low point in the fortunes of the Continental cause, drilled holes haphazardly into 40 kegs and fastened flint-and-steel firing locks inside of each. Short wooden pegs driven halfway through each hole from the outside made up a series of primitive contact fuses. The 40 kegs were filled with gunpowder and stoppered, then dumped into the Delaware to float willy-nilly downstream. The British held the lower end of the river, and all of the shipping at Philadelphia, the largest port in the country, either was British or British controlled, so it was reckoned that at least one keg might hit something and cause a panic.

One did, and it did.

It was a poor time for such a stunt. The ice had broken, and the river was filled with large chunks of it, so that the warships at Philadelphia, which ordinarily would have been anchored in midstream to discourage desertion, had been hauled out of harm's way to one shore or the other. Some boys saw the first keg to come along, and they rowed out in a small boat to examine it. The thing blew up in their faces.

The result was a considerable commotion, with British soldiers lining the Philadelphia shore, and marines on the warships banging away with their muskets at the kegs as they appeared. The marines and the soldiers must have been poor shots, or else the infernals were inferior, for all 39 of them bobbed on down the middle of the river and out to sea. No further property damage was done than the blowing up of a single rowboat, but the moral effect was great—on both sides. The British were more twittery than ever, while Francis Hopkinson— painter, poet, patriot, politician, composer, member

of Congress from New Jersey, and designer of the
Stars and Stripes—wrote a hilarious ballad about it,
"The Battle of the Kegs," which did much to cheer
the Continental soldiers that terrible winter at Val-
ley Forge. Not all victories are won on the field.

The next to turn his talents to the construction of
a submarine was another American, Robert Fulton.
His *Nautilus* was the first cigar-shaped one. It was
25 feet long, six feet in diameter, and was moved,
not very fast, by a stern propeller worked by four
men at a crank inside. A fifth man navigated it.
There was no conning tower, no periscope. The
navigator was supposed to take a good look at the
vessel he meant to attack, and then dive and go
under it.

Fulton never thought of his vessel as anything but
a ship-destroyer. The infernal was all the rage in
naval warfare, and sundry methods of delivering an
infernal from a small vessel to a large one had been
tried and found wanting. One method was simply to
push the thing toward the larger vessel, as Bushnell
had tried to do with his whaleboat near New London. Another was to ram the victim with a sort of
long run-out bowsprit to the end of which the infernal had been fastened. Still another was to try to
fasten it to the side or bottom by stealth. All of these
methods were as uncertain as they were perilous.
Fulton proposed a new one.

He would approach an anchored vessel—or at
least one that was motionless at the time—fairly
abeam. The small *Nautilus,* end-on, would not offer
much of a target. Before she could be hit, perhaps

even before she could be seen, she would dive. She would be trailing astern—by a prudently long cable—the infernal, which would be held up by floats. She would pass directly under the victim vessel amidships, surfacing at a good safe distance. The infernal would be slammed against the warship *on the other side* and would go off on contact.

This was the year 1801. Great Britain and France were at war. Napoleon planned to invade England, as everyone knew, and so the control of the English Channel was more important than ever. Fulton, an Irishman by ancestry, an American by birth, had lately been studying and working in England, but it was in Paris, France, that he built the *Nautilus*. Still, he wished to give the English the first chance. He crossed to London, where he failed to interest anybody in the idea—anybody, that is, who counted. The British would depend, as they always had, on their big ships, their big guns, and the stout-hearted men who handled these.

Fulton went back to France, where he interested Napoleon, who assigned a day on which Fulton could have the harbor of Brest to himself, allotted him a hulk to sink if he could, and appointed a commission to witness the experiment and to report.

To most men that experiment was an unqualified success. The *Nautilus* made her approach run, dived to a depth of 25 feet, and, after the explosion, came up, all unscathed, on the other side of the hulk. None of the crewmen (Fulton was not among them; he watched from the shore) had even been inconvenienced, though the vessel was submerged for more than an hour. And the hulk was sunk.

However, the commissioners, and after them Napoleon, decided that the *Nautilus* just wasn't fast enough. Even on the surface she had a hard time maintaining a speed of two knots, and she would be, Napoleon feared, a sitting duck for any warship from which she might be spotted.

Disappointed, Robert Fulton returned to America, where he tried in vain for several years to interest the new United States Navy in various underwater machines. At last he turned to the construction of the surface craft *Clermont* for the Hudson River run, and this, the world's first practical steamboat, was in every way a success—structurally, mechanically, and financially.

Desperation could be called the mother of invention. The building of submarines had always appealed to underdogs, to those who were waging a losing fight. It was natural, then, that in the Civil War the South, as greatly outnumbered by sea as by land, should dabble in submarine building.

It was in New Orleans that the first submarine privateer was built. She was to be a killer, like previous submarines. She would not take prizes, as any surface privateer would do, but would destroy enemy shipping by stealth. Her owners and operators would be paid, per tons sunk, by the Confederate States of America. Aptly named the *Pioneer,* she was a cigar-shaped thing 20 feet long, her greatest beam being three feet two inches. She carried a propeller at each end—one for coming, one for going—and these were turned by two members of the crew of three, who worked a crank. The third man manipulated a tiller. The *Pioneer* was fabricated of quarter-inch iron sheets riveted together, and she must have been mighty uncomfortable. Like Bushnell's *Turtle,* she was not designed to do any real fighting, only to get close to an enemy vessel unseen and fasten an explosive. She did blow up a barge in the still, shallow waters of Lake Pontchartrain, but when she was put into the river, preparatory to going down to the hunting grounds of the Gulf of Mexico, she sank; and that was the end of that.

The *CSS Hunley,* a primitive submarine made out of a 25-foot section of iron boiler four feet in diameter, had a tragic history. Time after time, while being tried out she had sunk to the bottom, usually with the loss of several lives. She was hexed, they said. Each time she was salvaged and refitted—but when at last she was sent against the *USS Housatonic,* largest of the Union warships blockading Charleston, South Carolina, it was clearly an act of desperation.

She rammed a bomb against the *Housatonic* and it went off, sinking the Union ship. This rates as the first successful submarine attack. However, the *Hunley* could not get away in time; her own plates were sprung by the explosion, and she was flooded and went to the bottom with all nine members of her crew. The blockade of Charleston continued.

The *Plongeur,* developed in France at about this same time, was a much larger vessel—146 feet long with a 12-foot beam. She was operated by an 18-horsepower compressed air engine and was moderately successful.

An Englishman, Garrett, made the first steam submarine in 1880. It had a collapsible funnel.

An Englishman also made the first electric submarine.

A French engineer, Goubet, in 1881 made for the Russian government several small electric submarines. They were 16½ feet long, cigar shaped, and 5¾ feet by 3¼ feet at their beamiest. Each was operated by two men. They carried no guns or torpedoes and were purely experimental.

The two greatest names in the development of the submarine, however, are those of the Americans Simon Lake and John Philip Holland. These were personal and professional enemies, often in litigation with one another, each an eccentric, irascible, opinionated small man of almost unbelievable persistence, almost diabolical ingenuity.

Holland was aiming at the U.S. Navy all the time, his purpose being to break Great Britain's supremacy at sea. But Lake had other ideas, and the craft with which he experimented in Chesapeake Bay were not military in their nature. They were rather exploratory, for each was supplied with wheels on which they could bump along the bottom—rather like an airplane, two large bow wheels and one small stern wheel.

If his grand idea came to nothing, if he was technically unsuccessful in the sense that he didn't make money, Lake will always be remembered for his pioneering. Not only did he come up with some new and novel ideas for hull construction, but he was the first to use a periscope and the first to develop an escape hatch. Moreover, he kept alive the conception of a commercial, nonmilitary submarine. It was his dream, and he clung to it.

Even now, while the *Lusitania* was plowing her grand way across the Atlantic, Simon Lake, in Bridgeport, Connecticut, was telling reporters that just as German submarines could strangle England to death, starve her slowly—it would take two years, he estimated—so only American-built submarines could save her. Surface vessels could not continue to break through that blockade much longer, he predicted. If he was promptly and properly backed, he said, within two years he could be turning out a series of cargo submarines, the only thing that could save the British Isles from destruction.

Holland, a small, nearsighted man with reddish drooping mustaches, was a New Jersey schoolteacher at the time of the Civil War. The duel between the *Monitor* and the *Merrimac* fired his imagination and turned him to the planning and building of submarines. He had a terrible time raising money, for he was looked upon as a crackpot, and he had no means of his own; but he kept at it. His first model was finished in 1875, but it was not until he had completed his ninth model, in 1898, that he got a customer. This *Holland,* as he called it, was 63 feet long with a 12-foot beam. It was operated—this was to prove Holland's most telling contribution to the cause—by electricity while submerged, by a four-cylinder gasoline engine rather like the engine of a Model T Ford while on the surface. The *Holland* was rated at 104 tons. The U.S. Navy ordered six of them at $170,000 each. Soon afterward Great Britain's Royal Navy ordered five. Holland was now affiliated with the Electric Boat Company of Groton, Connecticut, conveniently forgetting his prejudices.

Germany did not get into the submarine-building act until 1904. Since then she had made great strides —*how* great the world was about to learn.

Chapter 7

FOXY GRANDPA

THE CHILDREN in first class had their own dining room and their own playroom, located side by side amidships on C Deck. A stewardess trained in the care of small ones was in charge; but her services were not often needed because, in the first place, there were not many children in first class anyway, and, in the second place, many of those there had their own nurses or governesses with them.

The children in second class had a big playpen, a noisy, jolly place supervised by another specially trained stewardess, and *she* had plenty to do, for there were more children in second class than in both of the other classes put together, and there were no governesses or nurses.

There was no special place for children in third class, D Deck. There was no luxury in steerage, but who wanted it? Who expected it? The steerage ac-

48

commodations were, in fact, plain but comparatively spacious. In almost any other liner they could well have been mistaken for second class. The steerage passengers were not complaining.

To be sure, the five musicians were exclusively for the first classers. They played throughout every lunch and dinner in the big, balconied, white-and-gold dining room. Like any ship's orchestra, they specialized in so-called semiclassical music—tunes catchy enough to make you jiggle your fingers, arrangements fancy enough to include a great many grace notes, music that was not so soft as to cause you to stop talking to listen nor yet so raucous as to spoil your appetite. They did not play much ragtime, except on request. They mostly played genteel music, safe music.

The hit tune of the hour was "Memories," and they did this often. They also did "The Curse of an Aching Heart," "Moonlight Bay," "Can't You Hear Me Calling, Caroline," "A Little Love, a Little Kiss," "When I Lost You," and "When That Midnight Choo-Choo Leaves for Alabam," those last two being from the pen of young Irving Berlin, composer of that seemingly imperishable favorite—after four years, it was still in demand—"Alexander's Ragtime Band."

It could be that many of the Europeans in that sumptuous dining saloon occasionally expressed wonderment about why the orchestra always switched to "Just a-Wearyin' For You" or "The End of a Perfect Day" or some other Carrie Jacobs Bond composition at the entrance, noon or night, of a short, slight, sly-smiling, long-haired man who sat at the captain's table. Since he *did* sit at the captain's table, they might have reasoned, he must be somebody important; but, in heaven's name, *who?* To them he looked only odd, a bit impish on occasion, sloppy always. With the Americans it was different. They knew all about Elbert Hubbard, his ideas, his habits, his beliefs, his personal tastes—*he* saw to that—and so they knew as a matter of course that Carrie Jacobs Bond was his favorite songwriter. They might have guessed it anyway. And the musicians would know, too. They'd be told.

He was a phenomenon, this little man. There was nothing else like him in the world. It amused him to call himself—some said with a smile, others said with a leer—Fra Elbertus. He affected flowing ties and floppy hats, while his humor, always on display, was of the kind called homespun. He had opinions on everything—opinions he never hesitated to air. He was accompanied by his wife Alice, a plain, plump, steadfastly smiling woman, a former schoolteacher, who agreed with everything he said.

Hubbard had been born, almost 55 years ago, in Bloomington, Illinois, of parents presumed to be poor—or, if they had money, he would surely keep that fact quiet. Tufts College, Boston, recently had given him an honorary doctorate of arts, but his formal schooling never got beyond the elementary stage. He was a sensationally successful lecturer and author, his "Little visits to the homes of" books were to be found everywhere, while his *A Message to Garcia,* a pamphlet, was said to have sold 40,000-

000 copies. But he was much more than lecturer and author. He was a national figure, an ebullient and seemingly tireless spouter of aphorisms that were widely considered wise. He knew everybody. He was news wherever he went, whatever he said or did. At East Aurora, 16 miles from Buffalo, New York, he published a monthly magazine, *The Philistine,* which never failed to be provocative, and there, too, his 500-odd disciples hammered brass and tooled leather and bound books and otherwise labored to produce souvenirs for the tourist trade. Perhaps "pilgrimage trade" would be a more accurate phrase; for the folks who visited East Aurora did so to gawk, open-mouthed, at the Sage; *he* was the shrine.

Fra Elbertus had been buttonholed on A Deck Saturday morning, while the *Lusitania* was still tied to Pier 54, by reporters who experienced no difficulty in finding him. They asked if he wasn't afraid of a submarine attack, and he shrugged and grinned, mentioning the Big Lucy's celebrated speed. But why was he going abroad in wartime anyway? Again he grinned. He wanted to interview Kaiser Wilhelm, he replied. He had recently published a magazine article entitled "Who Lifted the Lid off Hell?" and had answered his own question with "William Hohenzollern." So the Kaiser might feel an urge "to make me look like a piece of Swiss cheese," but he'd take that chance. He smiled. It was doubtful that the Kaiser had ever even heard of Elbert Hubbard, but it made a good story.

"If he won't see me this time I'll wait until after

the war and visit him at St. Helena," the Sage had quipped, causing all the reporters to laugh.

There were other celebrities at the captain's table, as was the custom. There was Justus Miles Forman, a writer of romantic novels and short stories, a bachelor, man-about-town, member of the Century and Yale Clubs, who was going to Europe as a special war correspondent for *The New York Times*. There was Rita Jolivet, who had just finished a satisfactory run as the star of *What It Means to Be a Woman* and who had been for four years Otis Skinner's leading lady in *Kismet*. There was Charles Klein, a playwright, whose greatest success had been *The Music Master,* with David Warfield. He was preparing to write a stage comedy, *Potash and Perlmutter in Society,* with Montague Glass. There was Madame de Page of the Belgian Red Cross. There was George A. Kessler, sometimes called the Champagne King, a copiously bearded, cigar-smoking wine merchant from New York, who had some big London deals in mind and was carrying $2,000,000 worth of stocks and securities with him in his stateroom. There was Albert Gwynn Vanderbilt, when he consented to come.

But Elbert Hubbard—except when he listened, dewy-eyed, to one of the Carrie Jacobs Bond numbers—could and did outsparkle them all.

Chapter 8

IN THE BEST THEATRICAL TRADITION

THE WEATHER HELD on Monday, Tuesday, Wednesday; plenty of sunshine, the sea a lake. This made it the more ominous when the prebreakfast deck strollers on Thursday saw with a shock that the lifeboats had been run out. They now hung over the sea instead of resting by their keels on the boat deck, and the canvas covers had been peeled from them. Why this had been done in the predawn hours was not made clear. Perhaps as training for the deck hands. Or it could be from fear that the process might render the beholders uneasy, though surely here was a deed that could not be concealed. Most probably it was because at just that time the *Lusitania* passed into the war zone—that is, got within 500 miles of the south coast of Ireland. (German U-boats—*unterseebooten,* "undersea boats"— had a range of 5,000-6,000 miles, but this was not generally known, and anyway a line had to be drawn *somewhere*.)

The *Lusitania* carried 48 boats, of which 22 were standard lifeboats and 26 were collapsibles. The collapsibles were not suspended from davits but simply left on the boat deck, from which they could be shoved into the sea or, in the event of the ship's sinking, might float free. The regular lifeboats were hung eleven on each side, and were numbered from bow to stern, the even numbers to port, the odd ones to starboard. Both together, they were supposed to have accommodations for 2,605 persons —646 more than were aboard. Each member of the crew knew his lifeboat number; that was part of his training. Each passenger had been assigned to a lifeboat and urged to remember his number, but it is to be doubted that many did.

There had even been a lifeboat drill, as required by law. This was Tuesday morning. The crew members of a given boat—No. 13 this time—had been notified in advance, so that they were ready. At a whistle, they put on life jackets, ran to their boat, took the tarpaulin off and got in. That was all. They just sat there for a moment. They did not lift the oars or count them, or check the water and provisions, or start to swing the boat out. Then, at another whistle, they all took their life jackets off and went back to work. The passengers had not been required to do anything like this. They had not even been expected to watch, and only such first classers as had happened to be on the boat deck at the time had done so.

There were 2,325 life jackets, of which 125 were small ones for children. These were "Boddy's Patents," and they really were jackets, with armholes and tape fasteners at chest and waist. They were stowed in lockless boxes on the boat deck and there was to be found at least one—or two or three, depending upon the number of occupants—in each cabin. In each cabin, too, there was a small framed notice containing instructions about where the life jackets could be found, a picture of a man wearing one, and directions for how to put them on. A few of the passengers—but precious few—might have read those instructions and directions and studied the picture.

In addition, there were 35 life buoys—white-painted cork rings to which were fastened flares that ignited automatically when in water—at various places on the various decks, all outside.

When the ship entered the war zone, the lookouts were doubled. Instead of one man in the crow's nest and one in each of the ship's "eyes"—the starboard and port bows—two were to be stationed in each of these places, day and night, for the rest of the trip.

It is unlikely that many of the passengers were aware of the doubling of the watch, but none of them, even those in steerage, could fail to see that the lifeboats had been swung out. This was the real thing; this was it! Special drapes over all portholes and all smoking and lounge doors that opened upon a deck they had become accustomed to, since these had been used as a precaution against surface raiders all the way from New York. The outswung lifeboats struck, as it were, a more immediate note. They were almost like the clangor of an alarm bell.

None of this tingle of excitement was allowed to interfere with social plans for that Thursday, May 6—another day, incidentally, of perfect weather. The *Lusitania* was due to dock in Liverpool early Saturday morning, so that the next night, Friday, everybody would be packed or packing. Thursday night, tonight, was to be the big time. The ship's concert would take place then. The orchestra would hold forth with a special program. There would be announcements, greetings, the awarding of prizes. A group of singers in second class had promised to perform. So had the purser, James A. McCubbin.

McCubbin was a character, a beaming, white-bearded man with thousands of friends. He had been in the service for 35 years, as assistant purser or purser of most of the "ia" ships—*Etruria, Umbria, Carmania, Campania, Caronia, Franconia, Aquitania* —but this crossing was to be his last. He was 60 years old and about to retire. He had bought a little farm near Golder's Green, England, where he planned to spend the rest of his life. He was looking forward to it. He had been asked to perform at the ship's concert because he was an expert flute player. A good-natured fellow, he consented.

There were many private parties on this gala night, cocktail parties in staterooms. The most noteworthy of these was that given by Charles Frohman, the theatrical producer.

Here was a very great celebrity, a lion. Even people who had nothing to do with the theater craned their necks to get a peek at him, though he wasn't much to look at. He suggested a somewhat thick Napoleon, if Napoleon can be imagined with an Hebraic nose; yet his manner and way of living were anything but imperious. He never raised his voice. He seldom ceased to smile, even for a little while. The son of German emigrants, he was having a lifelong love affair with the theater. It was his wife, his mistress, his food, his drink. It was also a mighty good provider for him, though he was never much interested in money: the syndicate he headed, owned or controlled 60-odd theaters in England and the United States, and it put on about 500 shows a year. He was a great believer in the star system. They all worked for him—John Drew, William Gillette, William Faversham, Augustus Thomas, Gaby Deslys, Billie Burke, Julia Sanderson. . . . Ethel Barrymore had come down from Boston, where she was playing in *The Shadow* at one of Frohman's theaters, to see him off.

A shrewd manager, without ever seeming to be, Frohman was not in himself theatrical. He was not, that is, flamboyant or dramatic of appearance. "I have never known anyone more modest and no one quite so shy," James Barrie said about him, adding that Frohman "seemed to be born afresh every morning," so genuine, so childlike was his enthusiasm. He was greatly beloved. If he had any enemies they did not dare to speak up. He was known as a man who never broke his word.

He was credited, loudly, with almost singlehandedly raising the theatrical profession out of the murk into which it had been plunged when Lincoln was killed by a matinee idol, to the sunshine of respectability, decency and cleanliness. Frohman took the theater out of its barnstorming stage, its hambone stage, its rant. This might not have been strictly true—others, surely, participated in the great uplift—but everybody who worked for Charles Frohman, and there were thousands, believed it. To them he was more than just a successful producer; he was a god.

Fifty-four years old, he walked with a cane. It was his constant companion; he called it his "wife." Three years before, he had fallen on the porch of his home in White Plains and injured his knee. It turned into a terrible case of articular rheumatism. He was confined for six months to his city home, a suite in the Knickerbocker Hotel at Broadway and 42nd Street. He suffered horribly and had a hard time getting to sleep. As soon as he could, he hobbled the two short blocks to his office in the Empire Theater building, but he was never to walk again without a stick.

Reporters of course had interviewed him at the pier, and he had smiled off any fear of submarine attacks. One of those who came to see him, Paul Potter, a business associate and dear friend, asked:

"Aren't you afraid of the U-boats, C.F.?"

"No, I'm only afraid of the I.O.U.'s," replied Frohman, who loved to crack a nifty.

Like his friend Alfred G. Vanderbilt, the producer was devoted to the *Lusitania*. He crossed at least once a year and she was his favorite ship.

This time, again like Vanderbilt though for a different reason, he seldom was seen outside, but had his valet, William Staunton, bring most of his meals to his A Deck cabin, where he lay in agony. Still, it was only fitting that he should give a big party, no matter what the pain, in the old, smiling-with-a-broken-heart theatrical tradition.

Vanderbilt was at the party, though *he* probably didn't feel too jolly himself, having received, only two days before, a marconigram telling him that one of his oldest and closest friends, a classmate at Yale, Frederick N. Davis, had died suddenly in New York.

George Kessler was at the party, too, as indeed were all of those who had been invited to sit at the captain's table, including the captain himself.

Kessler asked Vanderbilt if he was going to England to do again the spectacular four-in-hand run from London to Brighton. Vanderbilt shook his head.

"No, there'll be no coaching for me this year. I'm sorry, but to drive a coach in these times is out of the question."

Captain Turner did not stay long at the party. A bellboy came to the door with a marconigram, and the captain stepped outside. It was from the British Admiralty. It read:

"Submarines active off south coast of Ireland."

They were having a high old time in there, laughing, chatting, drinking, but Captain Turner did not return to the party. Instead, he went to the bridge.

Chapter 9

LIKE A LAMB TO THE SLAUGHTER

CHARLES LAURIAT, JR., the book man from Boston, awoke Friday morning to hear the dismal honk of the foghorn. He got up, went to a porthole, shoved aside the drape. Yes, it was true. The fog was patchy, streamy, thin, but it *was* fog; and not only was the horn giving forth at regular intervals, but Big Lucy, as the pace-conscious Lauriat knew, had cut her speed. Lauriat knew, too, as an old traveler, that fog off the south coast of Ireland was by no means unusual. It would not make for good deck walking, and there would be no profit in straining the eyes for the first sight of land. After such blessedly sunny weather the fog was especially depressing. Lauriat shrugged, took a bath, rang for the steward, gave instructions to be waked before noon and, like a sensible man, went back to bed.

The night had been clear. The fog was not encountered until about seven o'clock in the morning.

Others besides Lauriat had noted the diminution of speed. It had been cut from 20 knots to 18, then to 15. There was much comment on it. Where was that last-minute burst of speed?

Though he would not let it show, Captain Turner was a troubled man. The message that took him from the Frohman party had been relayed from the naval wireless station at Land's End. It had been received at 7:50 p.m., and it was so vague and inconclusive that Turner wondered if it was complete; perhaps it was only part of a longer message, the rest of which had been lost. He asked to have it repeated. This was done, and that was all: "Submarines active off south coast of Ireland."

At 8:30 there came another message, this one addressed "To all British ships," a message that was to be repeated no fewer than seven times that night, indicating that the Admiralty was anxious. It read: "Take Liverpool pilot at bar and avoid headlands. Pass harbors at full speed. Steer midchannel course. Submarines off Fastnet."

Now here was something more definite. It is true that the Admiralty did not trouble to tell Captain Turner that U-boats had sunk a total of 23 vessels in these waters that week—since, that is, the *Lusitania* had left New York. Perhaps they feared to worry him? At any event, at least he now knew something.

Fastnet is a rock in the sea off Cape Clear, the extreme southwestern tip of Ireland. At the speed he was making, and the course he had ordered, Captain Turner reckoned that they would sight it at about 10 o'clock in the morning. That they did not was due to the fog, though some of the passengers who lined the port rail declared that they *had* in fact seen it faintly. It is certain that no submarine was seen.

The fog burned away, rather abruptly, a little after 11 o'clock. The result was a disappointment for the passengers, who had hoped to see land. There was nothing, not so much as a fishing smack— much less a patrolling destroyer. There were only the gulls, birds that had not been seen since Long Island was left astern, dirty white birds that rocked back and forth, screeching querulously, now and then diving into the wake for a morsel of garbage.

"Hell of a welcoming committee," more than one passenger muttered.

It was disappointing for the officers on the bridge as well. No sailing man likes to have to depend upon dead reckoning, and the officers had hoped that when the fog lifted land would be in sight, so that they could take a bearing on some familiar land-mark.

The absence of any other craft was eerie. Since the coming of the steamship, the south coast of Ireland had been England's lifeline, the route along which she got the greatest part of her food supplies. It was true, as the men on the *Lusitania*'s bridge knew, that the Royal Navy was being badly strained, what with crippling losses at the Darda-nelles, the necessity of guarding the main base at Scapa Flow, and the need to keep up the North Sea Patrol lest the German fleet break out; but even so, it might be supposed that they could spare to the

Irish Coast Patrol—that "Gilbert and Sullivan navy," as its own officers called it—something a little better than the handful of aged, obsolescent, small tubs that were stationed at Queenstown. Anyway, where were *they?* If there had been even one of them in sight when the fog lifted, however slow it might be, however rickety, the men on the *Lusitania's* bridge would have felt at least a little safer. But there was nothing. Only the gulls.

At 11:25 another message came:

"Submarines active in southern part of Irish Channel, last heard of twenty miles south of Coningbeg Light Vessel. Make certain *Lusitania* gets this."

Lusitania got it all right, but the message was not very helpful. Almost certainly Fastnet and Cape Clear had been left behind—the ship's course was presently 67 degrees East—and it was unlikely that they were yet anywhere near the Coningbeg lightship, which was anchored about halfway between Waterford and Carnsore Point, the southeastern corner of Ireland; but they could not be sure.

With the lifting of the fog the captain ordered speed picked up from 15 to 18 knots. His orders were to pass the mouths of harbors at full speed, it being the belief of the Admiralty that German submarines lurked off just such spots in order to be able to pick off vessels coming and going; and if the *Lusitania* was where he thought she was, they would be passing the Cork-Queenstown harbor in a couple of hours. Even with some of her boilers idle the *Lusitania* was capable of 21 knots. Turner did not order full speed ahead because such a pace would bring them to the mouth of the Mersey, to Liverpool, several hours ahead of high water there. The *Lusitania* drew 37 feet and she could only enter the Mersey at the top of the tide. If she arrived early she would have several hours to steam back and forth in the open Irish Sea, a dangerous spot.

Charles Lauriat got up a little before noon and went to the main lounge to see the noon posting of the last 24-hour run. It was 462, the lowest yet. After that Lauriat took a few turns around the deck before making for the big dining room on D Deck, at 12:40. There he was joined by his tablemate, a young Englishman named Lothrop Withington. They had struck up a warm friendship and were planning to continue it in London, where Withington lived.

The portholes were open. Lauriat especially noted this because he knew that the D Deck portholes were supposed to be kept closed and fastened while the ship was in a war zone. His seat was directly under an electric fan, and with the portholes open—and they were *all* open, on both sides: the dining room went the whole width of the ship—the draft was too much for him. As he had done on several previous occasions, this day he asked the table steward either to close a porthole or to shut off the fan. The steward shut off the fan, the easier process. Lauriat was to remember this.

At 12:40, just about this time, another marconigram was received: "Submarine five miles south of Cape Clear, proceeding west when sighted at 10:00 a.m." Well, that was all right. Wherever they were, they were well past Cape Clear by this time.

A little after one o'clock they raised land at last, but for some time they were not certain just where on the Irish coast it was. They edged closer, turning a little more north, for a better look. It was not until 1:40 that they raised what all of them recognized as the Old Head of Kinsale, a point that marked the entrance to Cork Harbor. It was unmistakable.

Still there was not another vessel in sight, though the sun was out, the air was clear, and they could see a long distance. The *Lusitania* had the ocean to herself—or so it seemed.

At lunch, in all three dining saloons, a wild story was going the rounds. Nobody knew where it had started, but it took many forms. The story had it that a submarine, or something like a submarine— one description of it was "with four towers"—had been spotted briefly to port, only a few hundred yards from the *Lusitania*. It had surfaced for only a moment, then immediately dived again.

Nobody took the trouble to carry this interesting information up to the bridge, so it was never officially recorded. The lookouts, clearly, had missed that show.

Far from creating a panic, the story was welcomed as a little excitement, for admittedly it *had* been a dull trip so far. The few who believed it assumed that what had been seen (nothing had, really) was a British submarine coming up for a better look, making sure that everything was all right with the *Lusitania*. This inspired confidence rather than fear. The Royal Navy did care, after all.

To make sure of the liner's position down to the last foot, Captain Turner ordered a four-point bearing to be taken. This is an elaborate operation and occupies the better part of an hour, during which time the ship must not alter speed or change course in the slightest way.

Before it was started, though, he did change course. He was too close in to shore. He had been ordered to steam in midchannel, but if he did that now he would be passing perilously close to the Coningbeg lightship, where a submarine had been sighted.

So he ordered the course changed to 87 degrees east, and the *Lusitania* veered away from the friendly coast of Ireland.

To Walther Schwieger, a blond, husky, good-looking German naval officer, who had been watching the Big Lucy for 20 minutes, this was almost too good to be true.

Schwieger had just turned 32, and this was his first command, this U-20. He had enjoyed reasonably good hunting, but they were tiny things he sank. He had never even dreamed of getting a shot at a huge four-stacker like this. Nobody else had ever dreamed of it either.

She was coming right toward him. He could not have hoped to catch her on her previous course, for she was very fast, but now she would pass within a few hundred yards of his forward torpedo tubes. Without turning away from the lens of the periscope, he ordered those tubes to be loaded.

The liner came on . . . and on. . . .

It was like a lamb being led to the slaughter.

"Ready, tube two?"

"Ready, sir."

A long, suspenseful moment. Then:

"Fire!"

The U-boat, motionless in the water until then, suddenly seemed to be kicked backward.

The torpedo was on its way.

Chapter 10

THE BIG BANG

LESLIE MORTON was a seaman and brand new as such, a young resident of New York City making his first voyage and getting a distinct thrill out of it. On the afternoon of Friday, May 7, 1915, a little after two o'clock, he was stationed as an extra lookout in the starboard "eye" of the *Lusitania*—forward on the main deck just behind the bows. Conscientious, he was scanning the sea. He saw a streak of white bubbles and whirled around.

"Torpedo coming on the starboard side!" he yelled up toward the bridge.

An instant later he was knocked down by the force of the strike.

"There's a porpoise," somebody on B Deck, on the starboard side, said offhandedly; and Mrs. Florence Padley of Vancouver, who had overheard, got out of her deck chair and went to the rail for a look, things being dull.

"That's no porpoise," she cried. "That's a torpedo!" And she ran for her cabin to get a life belt.

A scene painter employed customarily at Covent Garden, the famous London opera house, Oliver B. Barnard, standing at the starboard rail, saw something that just at first he took to be the tail of a big fish. An American woman, a stranger to him, asked him nonchalantly if that was a torpedo.

"I was too spellbound to answer. I felt absolutely sick. Then we were hit."

Carl E. Foss, a tall rangy physician from Helena, Montana, had specialized in the treatment of gunshot wounds, and he was on his way to England to offer his services to the British Red Cross. He was in the second class dining saloon, on D Deck, when what seemed to him "a big boom" sounded, jolting him—and everybody else. It was "a heavy dull sound, which was followed by a violent trembling of the ship fore and aft."

That second class dining room was crowded, and "the others seemed stunned, but there was no panic. ... The people all realized that something serious had happened."

To Dr. Moore, another physician in that same dining room at the same time, it was "a muffled drumlike sound coming from the direction of the bow."

(The second class dining saloon was far astern, as

though, the diners there complained, it was right smack over the propellers.)

Still another person present in that room, Miss Barrett, heard the strike as "something like the smashing of big dishes."

Lady Mackworth, daughter of a former Liberal member of Parliament and herself a prominent suffragette who was proud of having spent time in jail for the "cause," was just getting into the elevator in the first class dining saloon. To her the sound was no more than "a small thud."

Young Lauriat had finished lunch and was standing on the promenade deck well forward on the port side.

"Where I stood ... the shock of the impact was not severe; it was a heavy, rather muffled sound, but the good ship trembled for a moment under the force of the blow; a second explosion quickly followed, but I do not think it was a second torpedo, for the sound was quite different; it was more like a boiler in the engine room.

"As I turned to look in the direction of the explosion I saw a shower of coal and steam and some debris hurled into the air between the second and third funnels, and then heard the fall of gratings and other wreckage that had been blown up by the explosion."

A methodical man, he looked at his watch. It was 9:08. But that would be a.m. Boston time, for he had set his watch back as they steamed across the sea. It would be 2:08 p.m. here, in Greenwich time.

To Isaac Lehman, a New York export broker,

who was in the smoking room on A Deck, on the port side, it was "a noise like the boom of a cannon." He heard only one explosion.

Another Isaac, Isaac Jackson, of Paterson, New Jersey, heard it as "a rending, grinding sound rather than a sharp report." He too noted only one explosion.

To the wine baron, Kessler, who promptly went up to the boat deck, smoking a cigar as always, it was "a thud at the side of the vessel."

Theodate Pope of Farmington, Connecticut, a tall, slim, serene woman, by profession an architect, by avocation a communicator with the world beyond, was on her way to England to be a guest of Sir Oliver Lodge, with whom she wished to exchange spiritualistic chitchat. At the time the torpedo homed she was standing aft on A Deck. She was more poetical than Kessler.

"The sound was like that of an arrow entering the canvas and straw of a target, magnified a thousand times, and I imagined I heard a dull explosion follow."

Her companion, Edwin Friend, another noted hearer of voices from the beyond, cried: "By Jove, they've got us!"

D. A. Thomas, who had just finished lunch with his daughter, was another who heard only one explosion.

"We did not think much of it at the time."

Thomas was in the minority. Most of the passengers, in whatever class, and seemingly most of the stewards and sailors as well, knew instantly and as if it were instinctively—for they could hardly have been familiar with the experience—that the liner had been torpedoed from a submarine. It *couldn't* have happened; but it had.

Julian de Ayala, consul general for Cuba at Liverpool, returning to his duties, was ill in his bunk. He banged his head badly at the impact, and as he scrambled out he skinned one of his legs.

"I don't know how I got on deck. These English people are wonderful, so cool with no excitement. You would think nothing unusual had happened. Everyone followed orders."

Something unusual assuredly had happened, but not something unexpected. This, they told one another as, to a man, to a woman, they started toward A Deck—this was It.

Chapter 11

MAD MOMENTUM

KAPITANLEUTNANT SCHWIEGER, glued to his periscope, nodded approval. A perfect hit. He was 700 meters (765.8 yards, slightly less than half a land mile) away. He could see very clearly, though being submerged he could not hear much. The sound did not come as clearly to him, down his periscope, as it did to 15-year-old John J. Murphy, sitting on a stone wall near the Kinsale Light about ten miles to the port side of the *Lusitania*. John was there to watch the big ship go by, a popular pastime in those parts, as a small town prairie boy in the American Middlewest might go to the local railroad station to watch the daily flyer thunder past. To John the explosion was "a sort of heavy rumble like a faraway foghorn."

Schwieger saw the Big Lucy lurch to starboard, toward him; he saw a great column of smoke and steam; he saw her pitch low at the bows; and he knew that he wasn't needed in those parts any longer, and that it would be a good plan to get away from there before the rescue vessels appeared. There was no need for another torpedo. He could go home now, back to Emden.

The torpedo hit the *Lusitania* below the water line just under the No. 1 funnel, slightly abaft the bridge. It tore a huge hole in her almost-an-inch-thick steel hide, and then, after an agonizing split second of nothingness, there was a terrific inside explosion, probably one of the boilers. It was this that sent the terrifying, searing column of steam, soot, and metal up into the air, at least 150 feet above the tops of the funnels. A moment later all of this came raining down on the upper decks, along with many twisted gratings that had been ripped from their places. Fortunately there were very few passengers on those upper decks, most of them being in the dining saloons, their own cabins or the public lounges.

Lauriat, on deck far forward, had his shirt and his suit ruined. He noted, as did many others, that the noise and the column of dirty water were followed immediately by two separate, ominous motions of the ship. First she lurched to starboard, throwing many people off their feet and causing a great crash of chinaware in and near the dining saloons; then she dipped her bows a bit, as if she thought to dive under the sea right then and there.

"You could feel the two separate motions very distinctly. It seemed as if she were going down at once, but then she stopped suddenly as if the sea had met the water-tight bulkheads, and she seemed to right herself and even raise her bow a little."

The place where the torpedo had hit, while less than a third—scarcely more than a quarter of the distance—aft from the stem, still was nowhere near the place where the small arms ammunition was stowed. *That* was far forward, in the bows. Many of the passengers did not know this, however, and for a few moments there was a wild rumor that the popping sounds that followed the big blast were cartridges going off in all directions. They sounded, many said, "like Maxim guns." What they were, in fact, was the bursting of steam pipes. The rumor caused no panic, and passengers of all classes continued to make their side-tilted, slanting way to the upper decks without screaming or pushing.

The main steam pipe was among those broken. This meant that the giant liner would no longer answer her helm, for she was steered, of course, by power. Captain Turner, on the bridge at the time of the crash, promptly ordered her to be turned toward the coast of Ireland, where he thought it might be possible to beach her; but she plunged on to the eastward at almost 18 knots.

Captain Turner also ordered the engines to be reversed, his thought being to take some speed off the ship so that lifeboats could be lowered; but this, too, proved to be impossible.

Lauriat, despite his sooty condition, did not believe that he had time to change. He was convinced almost from the beginning that the ship would go down. The prospect did not frighten him, for he was an expert swimmer and in perfect condition, but he did wish at least to save some of his more important papers.

Near him, on A Deck, stood Mr. and Mrs. Elbert Hubbard. They were near the port rail, their arms were around each other, and they were beaming genially as though they found this whole affair good, clean fun. Lauriat advised them to go down to their stateroom—they had time: it was on B Deck, not far from his own—and get their life belts; but they just went on beaming.

He himself went below and strapped on a life belt. He was one of the few—the very, very few—who had taken the trouble to read the framed directions to be found in every cabin; so he knew how it was done. Then he went back up on A Deck, on the port side.

Mr. and Mrs. Hubbard, he noticed, were not where he had left them a little while ago. He never saw them again. Nor did anyone else.

B Deck, the level from which the lifeboats were to be boarded after they had been lowered from their davits on the boat deck, was the natural place for everybody to go. A few men from the engine room, grimy, frightening in their appearance, and themselves rather more frightened than were most of the passengers, made B Deck; but not many. Most of the Black Gang were doomed, and many were already dead down there. Also, there was a stir when a wild-eyed group of cooks and other kitchen workers came churning up from below. But there was no hint of panic. Nor did many of the passen-

gers charge the lifeboats. The general feeling
seemed to be, still, confidence in the *Lusitania*. She
couldn't sink; so why get excited?

There was a notable absence of able-bodied
seamen, real seamen. Many of these no doubt were
standing by for orders on or near the bridge or forward on the main deck. Others, too many others—
though this was not known at the time, on B Deck—
had been killed below in the first explosion, trapped
in a freight elevator. These were the men, together
with the *Lusitania*'s officers, who could have done
most to save lives. The kitchen help were worse
than useless; they were in the way. The stewards,
though theoretically subject to lifeboat drill, in
truth were no more than the grand-hotel employees
that they were supposed to be. The ordinary
seamen—as distinguished from the experienced
able-bodied seamen—were ordinary indeed; for most
practical purposes they were not seamen at all, only
day laborers, chippers of rust, swabbers of decks.

There were two attempts to get lifeboats over
into the water on the port side, something that no
veteran would have even tried for the ship was leaning so far to starboard that a portside boat would
have to be pushed or bumped all the way down to
the water. But men were desperate, and these two
attempts were made. The first boat broke loose entirely, tumbling its occupants, mostly women, into
the sea. Some but not all had life belts on. The other
boat miraculously made it, but it was less than half
full and had been so badly battered on the way down

that those who watched it from above for the most part were glad they were not in it.

Charles Lauriat went over to the starboard side to see if he could be of any help. Whatever launching was done would have to be done there.

And the *Lusitania,* that multimillion-tonned mass of momentum, surged furiously ahead.

Chapter 12

SAVE OUR SHIP!

THE ORDERLINESS with which diners in all three classes went topside was much commented upon at the time and later, but there was one luncher in the second class saloon who seemed to have gone mad for the speed he showed. This was Robert Leith, the chief wireless operator of the *Lusitania*. His "Marconi deck"—it was really a shack—was on the highest deck of all, the boat deck, but he was up there in a matter of seconds. He threw himself upon his instrument and started to rap out an SOS.

He said nothing about submarines because he didn't need to. Such a ship as the *Lusitania* does not go down in a lakelike sea without assistance. Though Leith did not name the *Lusitania* he did give, over and over, her International Morse Code designation, the letters MSU, familiar to everybody in the shipping world. And so he called for help, called again and again. . . .

Through the portside door of the shack he could see between davits the shore of Ireland, that famous landfall, the Old Head of Kinsale, and the sea between. There was not a boat in sight.

In a few minutes his power failed. The ship's generators had given out. He was prepared for this, and instantly switched on his emergency power storage batteries.

His finger on the bug hardly paused.

When the *Titanic* had hit an iceberg early in the morning of April 15, three years before, one of the most bitter things about that memorable night was the fact that her SOS—the first time those initials of distress had been used at sea, replacing the old CQD—though heard and answered by the *Carpathia,* 70 miles away, was not heard by the *California,* which was only from eight to ten miles away. The great *Titanic,* on her maiden voyage, and, like the *Lusitania,* considered "unsinkable," took two and three-quarter hours to sink. The sea was calm, the moon was up, and the *California,* if she had heard and had responded promptly, could have saved hundreds of lives. The reason she did not hear was that the law then did not demand that a ship's wireless be in operation around the clock, night and day. The *California*'s operator on that quiet night was sound asleep in his bunk.

Such was not the case with the *Lusitania.* Her SOS was picked up quickly, and in many places— among them, no doubt, Emden, Wilhelmshaven, and other stations operated by the Imperial German Admiralty.

There were three vessels not many miles southeast of the Big Lucy, though none was in sight. The nearest was the British tanker *Narragansett,* bound from Liverpool for Bayonne, New Jersey. She was about 35 miles from the *Lusitania.* A few miles astern of the *Narragansett* were the Leyland Line steamship *Etonian,* headed for East Boston, Massachusetts; and the *City of Exeter,* of the Ellerman Lines. These three were in wireless touch with one another, and all of them got the *Lusitania's* SOS. The three skippers instantly ordered a change of course to the northwest, each planning to pick up the Old Head of Kinsale by dead reckoning. Each ordered full speed ahead.

There was another, even nearer vessel, the *Swanmore* of the Johnson Line, only about 30 miles to the eastward of the Big Lucy, but *her* skipper, remembering the percentage of discretion to valor, and having no wish to run into a covey of German U-boats, had her put about and sailed back to Liverpool.

At the Old Head itself there was a wireless station that picked up the SOS. It was telephoned in to Queenstown.

There was a certain amount of resentment of the Cunard Line in Queenstown. The passenger liners no longer stopped there to coal on the eastward passage, as they had done for years until just the other day, and the Queenstowners were hurt. Aside from the fact that they were proud of their harbor, which has been called the most beautiful in the world, they missed the tourist rade.

No scintilla of this resentment showed in Queenstown the afternoon of Friday, May 7, 1915. When the news spread along the waterfront, every able-bodied man who had or could find for himself a place on any seaworthy craft that was available volunteered for rescue work.

The "mosquito fleet" consisted of something between 25 and 30 boats; nobody ever took the trouble to count them. The fleet included no Navy vessels— *they* stayed in port—and so there was no leadership, no chain of command, no organization. It was each boat for itself, whether tug, fishing smack, or mere harbor errand-runner. They swarmed out past Roches Point like bees out of a hive.

The starboard list of the *Lusitania,* which had been 15 degrees just after the torpedo hit, was growing more acute. It became 16 degrees ... then 17. . . . It became 20, and still the liner tipped. It began to look as if she might roll right over.

This list was started, of course, by the gaping hole torn in her side by the German missile, but it was made much worse when the starboard portholes of D Deck reached the water, which poured in through such of them as were open.

When Wireless Operator Leith looked through the port door of the Marconi shack now, he could see only davits and sky, no coast of Ireland. When he looked through the door on the starboard side he could see only davits and sea. The water was coming closer . . . and closer. . . .

He kept rapping out the SOS. The action had become automatic, requiring no thought, so that he was able to pray a little. He prayed that the ship would not go down. For Robert Leith couldn't swim a stroke.

Chapter 13

THE LAUNCHINGS WERE LUBBERLY

ALL OF THIS took place in a few minutes.

From the bridge came an order to such able-bodied seamen as were beginning to work on the lifeboat davits—not many—to desist and report forward. This they did, leaving the lifeboat job to amateurs.

Captain Turner was sure that his ship would stay float at least for a few hours, and once she had drifted to a stop it would be a simple matter, and a safe one, to launch all of the lifeboats on the starboard side. These, together with the collapsibles, should take care of everyone. By that time, too, rescue vessels could be expected from Queenstown.

Standing on the bridge, facing aft, the captain explained this in a clear, cold, loud voice to all who would listen.

"What do you wish us to do?" a woman called up to him.

"Stay right where you are, madam. She's all right."

"Where do you get your information?"

"From the engine room, madam."

That satisfied her, and she was silent.

Turner sent Staff Captain Anderson and other officers down to A Deck to move among the passengers with words of assurance.

Not everybody agreed with the captain.

Dr. Howard L. Fisher of New York, who was on his way to Belgium for the Red Cross, went to the port side and witnessed the smashing of one boat and the more or less successful launching of another. He joined Lady Mackworth and his sister-in-law, Dorothy Conner, there; and as he did so an officer came along shouting, "Don't worry! The ship will right itself!" As if calling him a liar, the ship a moment later took an angry lurch to starboard and pitched forward even farther.

A Mr. Thomas, who with his daughter at lunch "did not think much of it at the time," changed his mind and made for A Deck as fast as he could. A woman was standing on the rail, some ten feet above a swung-out lifeboat. "Let me jump!" she kept screaming. "Let me jump!" Nobody was touching her. "For God's sake, *jump!*" called Thomas; and she did, and then he did, and they were both saved.

The launchings were lubberly. In some cases the falls were simply hacked away with axes or with

penknives. Matt Freeman, amateur lightweight box-
ing champion of England, got his hand badly banged
on one of the davits. Madam de Page, who probably
knew in her heart that she would not survive but
wished to do all the good she could while there was
yet time, bandaged the hand.

The handling of the boats, once in the water,
likewise was lubberly. A few of the earlier ones
started for the coast when they were less than half
full, and all of them strove to get as far away from
the ship as possible, their occupants being afraid
that they'd be sucked down to the bottom of the sea
when the *Lusitania* at last did go down. Many were
overcrowded, if not at first then soon afterward; and
with a score or more of exhausted swimmers hanging on to the outside such a boat was likely simply
to founder. R. J. R. Mecredy, a young Dublin physician, saw one of them turn over three times, though
it was eventually righted.

F. Bertram Jenkins, the London manager of Cobb
and Jenkins, wool merchants, was sitting in the dining saloon having an after-lunch coffee with a
friend, Max Schwarez, and two ladies, when the
torpedo hit. They hurried up to A Deck, though
Schwarez somehow got lost on the way and never
was found. Jenkins and the ladies jumped into a
boat, but when this was halfway down to the water
(and here was a not uncommon occurrence on that
momentous afternoon) one end of it let go and everybody was tumbled into the sea. When Jenkins
came up (as not all of them did) he found that he
was *under* the boat, which had been turned upside

down. He got out and clung to the overturned boat, along with 20-odd other people. It didn't look too firm, and exhausted swimmers were joining them all the time, so Jenkins left it and struck out for an oar that was floating near at hand. He soon got a plank as well, but he surrendered this to two women who were barely keeping their heads above the surface by means of a deck chair. He found another oar, possibly the mate to the one he already had, but his strength was ebbing fast and he barely had time to work one oar under each arm when he fainted. He came to consciousness an hour and a half later in a fishing smack, more dead than alive—but sufficiently alive, at that, to ask if anybody had a cigarette. He never had finished his after-lunch coffee.

A physician, Daniel V. Moore of Yankton, South Dakota, ran up from the second class dining room in time to get aboard one of the boats. Something stuck, partway down, and the boat tipped on end, almost vertically, while the terrified passengers clung to their seats. A quick-witted sailor on deck seized a fire ax and chopped away the stuck fall. The boat landed in the water with a resounding spank, but it did stay upright. Frantically its passengers started to push themselves away from the *Lusitania,* which might go to the bottom at any moment now. Dr. Moore, however, had no faith in the craft. It had been badly sprung in the slap and was leaking; and it was overcrowded. So he picked up a keg and threw this into the water as far as he could, then dived in and swam to it. He was joined there by a steward named Freeman. After an hour and a half in the water they were picked up by the patrol boat *Brock*. Before he could catch his breath Dr. Moore was asked to set the fractured left thigh bone of one Frank Hook, a ten-year-old boy who himself had only just been pulled out of the water Dr. Moore did this; and immediately afterward the boy asked: "Is there a funny paper on this boat?" As it happened, there was not.

Many things were left unfinished when that torpedo so rudely interrupted the social life of the *S.S. Lusitania*. There was Jenkins' coffee, among others. W. G. Ellason Myers of Ontario was on the boat deck waiting for his opponent to come up from lunch for a promised game of quoits—a game that never was played. The virtually nonstop bridge game in second class among four enthusiasts, one of them a towering Episcopalian minister who was on his honeymoon, never was resumed after lunch, though the cards had been laid out, as had the pencils and score pads. Robert Timmons, a husky Texas cotton man, had just ordered a second helping of dessert, vanilla ice cream; but it never came.

Isaac Lehman, the new York exporter, was addressing himself to a highball in the smoking room on A Deck, on the port side, when the bang all but knocked it out of his hand. He put it down and hurried to his cabin on D Deck, having some difficulty wriggling his way past the others, who, understandably, were going up. Somebody had been in the cabin before him: the life belt was gone from its rack. Lehman pocketed his revolver; he didn't know why. On the way back up he encountered his cabin steward, Barnes, and complained to him about the theft of the life belt. Barnes got him another. In the B Deck lounge Lehman met the purser and the ship's physician, respectively James A. McCubbin the incredible flutist, and Dr. J. F. McDermott. McCubbin was an old man with white whiskers—it was he who had bought that little farm near Golder's Green, for he was retiring from the service while Dr. McDermott, clean-shaven, was young, being a substitute for the regular *Lusitania* physician, old Dr. James Pointon, who was laid up with rheumatism, an ailment that saved his life. But McCubbin and McDermott had at least one thing in common: they both thought it superlatively silly on the part of Isaac Lehman to push out in search of a lifeboat. The *Lusitania* sink? Don't be mad, man! He left them laughing at him. They were both drowned.

On deck Lehman found a seaman making fast a boat line that had been untied, and demanded to know why he was doing such a thing. Captain's orders, Lehman was told. He pulled out his pistol.

"To hell with the captain! Don't you see the boat's sinking? Now you untie that!"

He was obeyed.

The boat, mishandled as usual, swung inboard, knocking people down on the deck. When it was swung out again Lehman and a lot of others started to get aboard. Lehman had one foot on the boat and one on the ship's rail when the boat was swung out even farther. He fell in the middle and splashed into the nearby sea.

Though his right leg hurt horribly—it might have been broken, it felt like that—he was so afraid of being caught in the suction that he swam as hard as he could for four or five hundred feet before he turned to look back, just in time to see the *Lusitania* go down.

"It sounded like a terrible moan," he said.

That was exactly 18 minutes after the torpedo had hit.

Chapter 14

LIKE ANY OTHER MAN

THERE WERE SEVERAL HUNDRED more life jackets than people aboard the *Lusitania,* but you would not have believed it that afternoon on the boat deck. Most of the lifeboats—all of those on the starboard side—either had been launched, with whatever success, or had been lowered to the level of the B Deck rail below, since it was from there that they were meant to be loaded. This made the presence on A Deck of several large boxes on which was stenciled LIFE JACKETS the more conspicuous. Each was about the size and shape of an American coffin or casket.

(At least one of these coffinlike containers was to float off and itself serve as a lifesaver. A tired fireman, without a life belt or other floating aid, saw it and swam gratefully to it. When he opened it and prepared to climb in he was startled to see that it was already occupied—by a woman. "Got room for one more?" he asked. She nodded weakly, and he wriggled in. For two hours, side by side, wet and unhappy, they lay there in that awkward canoe, until they were rescued by a fisherman.

These boxes were quickly emptied, and "Where'll I find a life jacket?" was being asked right and left.

"In your stateroom, of course," the more sensible ones said.

"Oh."

This was very well for first classers, most of whose cabins were on A or B decks, or on C Deck, though a few, like Lehman's, were on D Deck. But members of the other two classes and of the crew had quarters on E Deck or below, and often these were far forward instead of amidships or aft, as was the case with so many first class accommodations. E Deck and all the starboard side of D Deck almost from the beginning had been unreachable because of the sharp list and the open portholes.

This was the only touch of discrimination, if it could be called that. Nor were all the first class passengers taking advantage of it. Edward Gorer, to name only one, easily got his life belt from his boat deck cabin, but he gave it to a woman, a Miss Josephine Brandell, who was unable to get to her own; and she was saved, Gorer was drowned.

Most of those who did have life jackets didn't know how to put them on. They had been living for almost a week in rooms which had a careful list of instructions framed on the wall, but they had not paid these any attention; and now they were confused. Charles Lauriat noted this.

"In their hurry they put them on every way except the right way; one man had his arm through one armhole and his head through the other; others had them on around the waist and upside down; but very few had them on correctly. I stopped these people and spoke to them in a calm voice and persuaded them to let me help them on with the belts, for they certainly stood no show in the water rigged as they were. At first they thought I was trying to take their jackets from them, but on reassuring them they let me straighten them out."

Lady Mackworth, who had been looking everywhere for her father, D. A. Thomas, who was looking everywhere for *her,* dared to go to her cabin on B Deck. So far off-center was the ship that she had to walk with one foot on the wall, or bulkhead, the other foot on the deck. This required watching her feet, and she was startled when she bumped into a similarly engaged stewardess going in the opposite direction. The stewardess, too, was startled. They both began to apologize, and then, with a little giggle at the realization of the precious time that they were wasting in politeness, they broke apart and continued their separate ways. Lady Mackworth got to her cabin, and got her life jacket. She went to her father's cabin next door and got his life jacket as well. She went back up to A Deck. She put on one life jacket and gave the other to somebody else. She was afraid of the boats and wanted to jump into the water, but she was afraid to do that, too. It looked so far down there! She might have fainted, standing up. The next thing she knew green sea water was swirling around her ankles, then around her knees. She didn't need to make up her mind; the Atlantic Ocean had made it up for her.

"I suddenly felt the water all about me and was terrified lest I should be caught in something and held under. I went right under a long way, and when I came to the surface I had swallowed a lot of water before I remembered to close my mouth tight. I was half conscious but managed to seize a boat which I saw in front of me, and hung on to it. I lay on my back, supported by my life belt, with the boat in front on me. The water was crowded with wreckage and people swimming. There were some boats not very far away and we called to them, but the people in them could not hear us."

She was in the water two hours and 45 minutes, a good deal of the time unconscious. Then she found herself opening her eyes. She was on the deck of a Queenstown tug, the *Bluebell*. A sailor grinned at her. "You're better now," he said.

A little farther astern, and thus not swept away quite so soon, was a little group composed of Rita Jolivet, the actress, her brother-in-law George Vernon, Captain A. J. Scott, a British Army officer en route from India to England by way of the United States, and theatrical producer Charles Frohman. Frohman, still leaning on his "wife," was unperturbed, and even smiled a little. He knew that it would be useless for him, in his rheumatic condition, to try to get into one of the boats, and the others thought it too risky, a lifeboat being a perilous place at that stage of the wreck; so they just stood there, waiting for the end to come.

"Why fear death?" said Frohman. "It is the most beautiful adventure in life."

He was quoting from his friend James Barrie, whose *Peter Pan* he had himself produced. Captain Scott got a life belt for him and made him put it on, but Frohman soon took it off again and gave it to "an hysterical woman." Soon after that the big wave came, carrying them all away. A badly battered Rita Jolivet was the only one who survived to tell the story. She clung to the overturned boat against which she had been thrown.

Justus Miles Forman, the novelist-clubman, and Charles Klein, the playwright, who were also of this group, though not immediately with them at the end, were washed away in a similar manner. *Potash and Perlmutter in Society* would never be written.

Theodate Pope, her maid Emily Robinson, and her spiritualistic companion Edwin Friend decided not to wait and be carried ignominiously off. Each wore a life jacket when they jumped from the B Deck rail—first Friend, then Theodate, then the servant. Theodate wondered as she fell whether Emily Robinson would be afraid to follow her. She was slammed up against something—a boat, she thought—and she was sure that she was about to die. Then something heavy fell on her head; she never did learn what it was, but she could feel it crush the straw hat she wore. That was the last thing she knew for a long time. She was at length rescued, and so was the maid, but Edwin Friend was called away to examine at first hand that world after death in which he so passionately believed.

Perhaps the calmest and quietest person in the afterdeck throng, and certainly one of the most effective, was Alfred Gwynne Vanderbilt. Dapper, as always, he pitched in to do whatever he could, by his very manner inspiring confidence. There is an old American saying that it takes four generations from shirtsleeves to shirtsleeves, but Alfred Gwynne had shown no sign, until this time, of emulating or reverting to the characteristics of his great-grandfather, the renowned Cornelius, founder of the fortune. He had shown, on the contrary, a positive aversion to work. Why should any man work if he happened to have a hundred million dollars? Yet this day at sea he covered himself with glory. It could be said of him, as Malcolm said of the Thane of Cawdor, that nothing in his life became him like the leaving of it. For he was doomed.

Vanderbilt was fond of the Big Lucy and had crossed on her many times. He had sailed in his yacht down New York Bay to greet her off Sandy Hook at the end of her first voyage, when she took the speed record away from the Germans, so he could be said to have seen both the first and the last of her.

"Find all the kiddies you can, boy. We want kiddies," he told his valet, Ronald Denyer, who obediently went below to look.

Vanderbilt helped women get into the boats. He helped them fasten their life jackets. He soothed them when they waxed hysterical, as a few did. And he never raised his voice.

His own life jacket he took off, giving it to a nursemaid. This called for real courage. There weren't any more jackets for the taking now, and young Vanderbilt, though he was an expert at four-in-hand driving, automobile racing, polo and other fast sports, never had learned to swim.

He owned the Vanderbilt Hotel in New York, valued at about $3,000,000. He owned 11,300 shares of New York Central, 28,110 shares of Pittsburgh and Lake Erie, 10,110 shares of Pullman, 2,500 shares of North Western preferred, 1,000 shares of New Haven, 700 shares of Northern Pacific, 1,400 shares of St. Paul, 200 shares of Lincoln National Bank, 1,000 shares of the Chemical National, 700 shares of National City, and sundry assorted holdings; but he drowned like any other man. So did the valet.

Chapter 15

"SHE'S GONE!"

THE DIN WAS EARSPLITTING. Most of the people had been admirably quiet on deck, but once in the water their lungs, it would seem, expanded, and how they yelled! The screams carried over the crunch and splintering of timbers, the bang of oars, the multitudinous splashing. The only ones who were silent were those who lay exhausted at the bottom of boats, or, those in the water, the dazed and the dead, bumping about like logs.

Two sturdy steerage passengers, Mr. and Mrs. N. M. Pappadopoulo, declined to trust either boats or life belts. Instead, they stripped and dove, after which they started, with long strong brave strokes, to swim for the coast of Ireland, ten or eleven miles away. Mrs. Pappadopoulo was in a stupor of weariness when the first of the mosquito fleet vessels picked her up a couple of hours later. Her husband had disappeared, his body never was to be found.

It was just not Matt Freeman's day. After getting his hand bandaged he returned to the job of helping women climb into boats. When he saw that the end was near he went to the extreme stern, still high out of water, climbed the rail and dove. He made a good dive; but somehow an overturned and partly submerged lifeboat got in his way at the last moment, and he took a hard crack on the head just before he went under. He felt no pain, but he knew as soon as he came up that he was bleeding badly; blood ran down over his face. Like everybody else in the water around him, what he most feared was to be too close to the *Lusitania* when it sank, for it seemed certain that the vortex would be a powerful one. So Freeman swam swiftly away, though he was getting weaker with every stroke. For a little while he disputed with several other desperate men the possession of a keg that would have upheld no more than two of them; but he was so weak that he broke this off—he, the champion!—and tried elsewhere. He finally got hold of another overturned lifeboat (or could it have been the same one?), to which, with many other men and women, he clung for almost three hours. Again and again in that time he was tempted just to let go, as others were doing. But he hung on, and in time was rescued, living to fight again another day.

S. L. B. Lines of Toronto was lucky. After seeing his wife aboard an already overcrowded lifeboat, he worked off his shoes and dived over the rail. For all the appalling litter in the water, he hit nothing. He had no life belt on when he dove, but somebody, he never did learn who, threw one to him; and in ten minutes he was hauled aboard a boat.

Michael G. Byrne, of 444 West 50th Street, New York City, a retired merchant and a former deputy sheriff of New York County, was in the water for more than two hours, and there were times when he literally swam between rows of floating bodies. He wore a life belt. He worked the rings off his fingers and put them into a coat pocket. Several times his steamer cap was knocked off, but he was always careful to recover it and to put it back on. He was afraid of catching cold.

Charles F. Lauriat, Jr., was a methodical man, a looker-ahead. When he had done all he thought he could for the life jackets of those who mulled around on A Deck, he took a look down at the water and calculated that he would have time to make one more quick trip to his cabin. He already had his cash pinned to an inside coat pocket, but he wanted to get his passport and some personal business papers. He knew, of course, exactly where these were.

His cabin was on B Deck, far forward, and as he walked along the main passageway, his legs widespread as those of Lady Mackworth had been a little earlier—it was rather like wading through thigh-deep water or scuffling along the rails of a narrow-gauge railway—he passed many cross corridors on the starboard side, each of them ending in a porthole. Most of the portholes, he noted grimly, were open. The water was only a few feet below them now. Soon millions of gallons of it would be pouring in. Lauriat did not have time to shut them; and, besides, the damage was already done on the lower decks.

His cabin was an inside one, having no port of its own, and when he threw the light switch nothing happened; the ship's generators had long since ceased to function. However, it was his habit to keep a box of matches near his bunk in case he woke in the night. He felt for this and found it, right where it should have been. Soon he had the papers. He must hurry now. He noted again, as he went back to the stairway, that those portholes were still open.

There were still two lifeboats on the starboard side, at the B Deck level. Each was filled with women, and each was in trouble. The more forward one, which Lauriat could not reach, was free from its lines but had got itself fouled by a funnel stray, while the funnel itself, almost parallel with the water (so great was the list) hovered just above it, a frightful Damoclean sword. That funnel was big enough to drive a horse and carriage through, as advertisements and Sunday feature stories were so fond of pointing out, and if it ever collapsed upon the boat it would infallibly squash to death everybody there. Fortunately it did not collapse—none of the funnels did—and the boat got free.

Lauriat turned his attention to the other boat. So low in the water was B Deck that this second boat was actually afloat. But she was still fastened to her davits, forward and aft. When the ship went down— and it must be only a matter of minutes now—the whole boat and everybody in it would be taken to the bottom. Lauriat climbed into the nearer end, the stern, and unfastened the fall there. Forward, a steward was hacking at *his* line with a pocket knife. If he'd only had an ax! Lauriat wanted to help him but it would have taken too long to work his way the length of that boat, cluttered as it was with women, oars, kegs and the like. Besides, just at that moment he was struck in the back of the neck by the downarched davit end. The boat was up to the level of A Deck now. That's how fast the *Lusitania* was sinking.

Yelling for everybody to follow him, Lauriat jumped into the sea. He swam furiously for about 100 feet, then turned.

Something slithered down over his head to his shoulders and started pulling him underwater. He fought it, wondering what it was. He thanked the older kids at Camp Asquam, Maine, where as a small boy he had been wont to summer, for their then-obnoxious ducking activities. Many times young Lauriat had been forced down "to see Susie the Mermaid," and held there for a long time.

At last he got free. He learned that what had entangled him, almost costing him his life, was the wireless antenna of the ship, strung between topmasts. He was glad to get rid of *that*.

He got his head up in time to witness the actual sinking.

"My God, the *Lusitania*'s gone!" cried George Kessler, who was floating nearby.

They all felt that way. It was true, though it was impossible, just at first, to believe.

There was no dramatic upheaval of the stern, no threshing of exposed propellers. This might have been because the *Lusitania* was in comparatively shallow water—360 feet—less than half of the *Lusitania*'s own length, so that the bow could have touched bottom some time before the bulk of the ship went under, letting her down easy.

One moment that enormous floating luxury hotel was there; and the next moment it wasn't.

Chapter 16

ENOUGH DAMAGE

"SHE SLIPPED DOWN as if she was gliding down a greased surface," was the way Michael Byrne put it.

This is not to say that there was silence. There was a terrible hissing of steam and splashing of water. There were shouts of rage and screams for help. There were groans, curses, prayers. There was the splintering of wood, the screech of violated metal. It was pandemonium.

And over it all, like a blanket of sound, was the peevish call of gulls.

The vortex that everybody expected, and dreaded, the whirlpool, the irresistible suction, did not develop. On the contrary, as all viewers agreed, the *Lusitania,* when she sank, threw up into the air a tremendous mass of steam, water, soot, smoke and

104

millions of small articles such as boxes, barrels, benches, deck chairs, cushions, crates. . . .

For a whole minute afterward these objects were splashing into the water all around, a veritable hail of them. Many people were hurt this way, and perhaps some were killed. It was impossible to tell at the time which bodies were without life and which were only unconscious, there were so many of them.

The reason for this huge upheaval, this terrific shower, as every engineer must have seen, was the boilers. When the *Lusitania* went under the four funnels, almost horizontal by that time, gulped in vast drinks of sea water, thousands of tons of it, which doused the still-hot fires, causing a head of steam that lifted every loose thing into the air.

At least two swimmers, a man and a woman, were separately sucked into funnels and then spewed out again with the steam.

The woman, picked up soon afterward, was utterly black from head to toe. Her eyeballs were the only white things about her. Her name was Margaret Gwyer; she was a minister's wife who had been in second class. The men who pulled her out of the water thought, for a moment, that they were rescuing a Negress. Her own husband, when they were reunited an hour or so later, did not recognize her.

The man—a man called Pierpont, from Liverpool —was seen as he was sucked in, and seen again, a moment later, when, black as the ace of spades, he was spat out again. He was scared but not crippled.

As fast as he could go, he started to swim away from what remained in sight of the *Lusitania*.

The person who saw this happen to Pierpont was one of the least conspicuous of the survivors, Captain Turner, who was clinging to a chair. He had stayed with his vessel to the end, in the old tradition. He did not leave the bridge until it was awash, and then only to climb up the signal halyards. He truly believed himself to be the last living person aboard the liner (in fact there were still a few left at the extreme stern, but Turner did not know this), and when he saw an oar floating nearby he quit the mast, struck out for it, and reached it. The chair came along a little later and he abandoned the oar for it. Though he was in uniform, including his cap with its gold braid, he was not recognized in the hullabaloo until dusk, several hours later, when a seaman on a raft spotted him and rescued him. He had been in the water almost three hours. He was 63 years old.

There were heels, of course, that afternoon. There are always heels. A few of the lifeboats started for shore when less than half full. But most of the men worked long and hard, worked until their arms felt like falling off, right on into the darkness.

Nobody got paid for this, or expected to. Nobody was going to win any sort of award. It was just a matter of being human.

Leslie Morton and William Parry, a couple of ordinary seamen who were not really ordinary —Morton, still in his teens, was on his first voyage— surely did far more than the call of duty might demand. Working out of a collapsible, the two husky lads were credited with saving, between them, about 50 lives. Not many people ever have a chance to do that.

Morton was the lookout who had first seen the torpedo coming. Later he and Leith, the wireless operator, who was plucked unconscious out of a half-submerged lifeboat, were to be thanked personally by King George V.

Kathleen Kaye, barely 15, and no giant, comforted the stricken like any level-headed matron. She lifted several people into the lifeboat in which she found herself, and when one of the sailors fainted from exhaustion she calmly took his oar and pulled for him.

Gerta Neilson, a milliner from third class, fell out of an overcrowded lifeboat, and she didn't have a jacket on. John Welsh, one of the few engineers who survived, dived in and brought her back. She was grateful. It marked the beginning of a romance. Exactly a week later, May 14, they were married in Manchester, England, his home town.

So—the *Lusitania* was gone; and what remained, besides the bodies of living and dead alike, was a broad, widespread mass of debris. A great deal of this was sharp stuff, dangerous to bump into, especially as darkness approached. Very little of it, as Isaac Lehman, clinging to his oar, glumly remarked, was *large* wreckage, the kind that might have been useful. Lehman was a pretty large piece of wreckage himself, with his possibly broken right leg. He weighed more than 200 pounds, had all his clothes on, and presumably still carried that pistol. It took six men to haul him aboard, when at last he was picked up by a lifeboat.

The air grew cooler, and so did the water. After the first shock there was little screaming, and no mad wailing. But as the shocked, shivering survivors waited to be saved there was whimpering, and there were moans.

A wild rumor went the rounds. They were being carried out to sea by currents. They would never be rescued. There wasn't a breath of truth in this, but it was widely believed, even by seamen who should have known better.

At about five o'clock a few of the more watchful ones—most had been staring in the opposite direction, toward Ireland—sighted two steamers approaching from the south-southeast. Smoke was pouring out of their stacks, and seemingly they were moving at full speed—and right for the scene, as though with a real purpose. Excitement ran high.

Then abruptly, without having given any kind of sign or signal, the two ships changed their course to south-southwest. In a very short time they were out of sight.

Kapitanleutnant Schwieger had only one torpedo left. He fired this at the leader of the three vessels steaming to the assistance of the *Lusitania* survivors —that is, the *Narragansett*. He missed—he was to record in his log that he thought the steering mechanism of the torpedo was faulty—but by no more than a few feet, badly scaring the skipper and hands of the *Narragansett,* who had seen the line of bubbles.

The skipper jumped to the conclusion, and his mates agreed with him, that the SOS had been a trap, that the Germans themselves, those demons, had sent it. The *Narragansett* swerved swiftly and zigzagged away from the coast of Ireland.

This change of course was not noted from the *Etonian* and the *City of Exeter,* which were some miles astern, but what was noted was the U-20—it could have been none other, though Schwieger made no mention of this incident in his log—which surfaced right between these two vessels, scaring both skippers into altering course suddenly, as the captain of the *Narragansett* had done, and heading away from Ireland and from the poor, soaked, bobbing survivors. Schwieger chased them, doubtless hoping that he could destroy them with his deck gun, since he was clear out of torpedoes, but with their safety valves fastened down they outpaced him by two knots, even when he was on the surface. In a little while he broke off the pursuit and headed for the entrance to the Irish Sea and the long voyage home. He had done enough damage for one day.

Chapter 17

THE LADY WHO CHEWED GUM

QUEENSTOWN WAS NOT unaccustomed to wrecks. Situated in Cork Harbor on the south side of Great Island, it had been called Cove of Cork until 1849 when Queen Victoria landed there, the first time she set foot on Irish soil. It had been a fishing settlement for as far back as the records went and its residents were attuned to the sea and its vagaries. Never before, though, had they been faced with anything like this.

Because of the mild climate and the beautiful bay, Queenstown had lately developed into something of a tourist town. There was no particular season; people came and went at all times of the year. This meant that the town had rather more hotel accommodations than could be expected in a place of similar size, ordinarily, in that part of the world.

Queenstown was also a naval base, headquarters of the Irish Coast Patrol. The local fleet, complete in harbor on this May 7, 1915, consisted of four small cruisers, *Juno, Isis, Sutley* and *Venus,* all antiquated. They were under the command of an admiral, H. L. A. Hood, who was also antiquated. Why weren't they out, patrolling the south Irish coast as they were supposed to do? Because Admiral Hood did not believe that any one of them could stand up to a German sub, and many such subs had been reported as seen in the nearby bays and coves. The cruisers had only slow-firing six-pounders. So he kept them at home. He did not even send them out after the news had come of the sinking of the *Lusitania.* The mosquito fleet vessels could take care of that.

There were many bars, or public houses, in Queenstown, and upstairs over one of these was located the small, badly lit office of Wesley Frost, the United States consul. The job did not amount to much, now that the big liners had ceased to put in at Queenstown. To Frost, intensely sympathetic to the British cause, this disaster meant war—war, that is, between the United States and Germany. He knew that there had been many Americans aboard the *Lusitania,* and if any of them were killed he did not see how even the peace-at-any-price secretary of state, William Jennings Bryan, could hold out against the rage that would rise from the American public.

There were some telephones in Queenstown—not many—but Frost had one of them. By means of this he verified the report. Then he set out to meet J. J.

Murphy, the local Cunard agent, and see what he could do.

Murphy, though stunned, already had gone into action. He sent a wireless message to the London office. He made hotel accommodations. He informed the hospital and also each of the physicians in town. He promised clothing dealers that the Cunard Line would underwrite the purchase of any wraps the survivors, whether male or female, might need. He asked the Naval Reserve men to get out their stretchers. He arranged for tea and whisky, and for food as well. He alerted the undertakers. It would be a big night for the undertakers.

Meanwhile, the mosquito fleet was setting forth, helter-skelter, in no special order. It was joined, just outside the harbor, by a Greek coaster, the *Katerina,* which had received the *Lusitania*'s SOS and had been heading in that direction anyway. The *Katerina,* though small as a steamer, undoubtedly was the biggest vessel in the mosquito fleet. The most familiar vessel, perhaps, was the side-wheeler *Flying Fish,* which for many years had acted as a tender to the big ocean liners when they still condescended to put in at Queenstown. Many of the craft in this thrown-together fleet were dependent upon sail, but the *Flying Fish* at least had a boiler, a fire. Many of those out there would need a fire.

Flying Fish was only her official name. Among Queenstowners she was usually called the "Galloping Goose." She was no thing of beauty, but she was steady and could be useful.

Hundreds of people from miles around made their

way to the narrow Kinsale Old Head, the nearest land point to the place where the *Lusitania* had gone down. They watched the mosquito fleet tumble out, and in the failing light to the south they could see the first of the *Lusitania*'s lifeboats coming in.

Six of those lifeboats, numbers 1, 11, 13, 15, 19 and 21—all, be it noted, starboard side boats—were to reach Queenstown under their own power. The other 16 either were never launched or were overturned or so battered that they could serve only as rafts for the desperate.

The six lifeboats that did make it were for the most part tolerably well filled, though in that placid weather it would have been possible to overload them without serious risk. None, however, had a single man hanging to the looped ropes outside of the hull, ropes that had been put there for that very purpose. Many more lives might have been saved if these were used.

The collapsibles were a different matter.

These were not inflated rafts, as the name might seem to imply. They were flat, keeled, wooden boat bottoms equipped with collapsible wooden seats and collapsible canvas sides. They had no davits or other means of fastening, and they simply lay on the boat deck, A Deck, underneath the regular lifeboats. Each in its collapsed form occupied only about a third as much space as a full lifeboat. There were 26 of them, as compared with 22 lifeboats. They were supposed to float off the boat deck in the event of a wreck, and many—perhaps most, conceivably all— did this. One trouble was that the sides and the seats worked together, so that the seats could not be set up without raising the sides and vice versa. The inconvenience of this became apparent when wild-eyed swimmers frantically clutched a half-raised side and refused to let go even for a moment, no matter what the would-be rescuer inside of the half boat-half raft might say. This happened time and again. Also, the oars would float off, and the wooden pins for holding the seats in place were often missing.

In any kind of sea these contraptions would have been nothing better than rafts, and not notably stable rafts, either. However, the Atlantic Ocean off the south of Ireland that balmy afternoon was no more than a millpond; as for oars, the water was full of them. There were at least as many oars floating around as there were deck chairs. So that the collapsibles, in the hands of determined, not easily dismayed men, proved to be mighty useful.

Leslie Morton and William Parry, for instance, the two heroic crewmen, used an assembled collapsible in their major operation, saving some 50 lives. Charles Lauriat, once he got rid of that wireless aerial, made for a collapsible and, with the aid of a couple of husky volunteers, despite a great deal of exasperation, soon had it filled with dripping victims.

These included a man named McMurray, from Toronto, who, when first seen and hailed, was seemingly striking out alone for Ireland, as Madame Pappadopoulo had started to do. He changed his mind, however, and gladly climbed aboard. He had a bad chill, he said; but once this had somewhat subsided he was to prove a tower of strength at the oars.

Lauriat and his associates deposited their boatload of victims on a fishing smack about halfway to shore; they were later transferred to the much more comfortable *Flying Fish*. The last one to join Lauriat's crew, just as they were about to break away from the tangle of floating wreckage, was the lady who chewed gum.

"Won't you take me next, please?"

Lauriat, who was standing in the stern with a steering oar, whirled around. The woman who had called was not more than ten feet away. Only her head was visible, for she was entirely encased in jagged bits and pieces of debris.

"I can't swim, you know," she added.

She was smiling a little, and—she was chewing gum.

Lauriat deliberated. To back the boat to her would mean disturbing the wreckage. That might injure her. It might even cause her chin to slip off the board upon which it was resting and which appeared to be the only thing that was keeping her on the surface. So she would be lost before they could grab her.

"Stay right where you are," he called. "I'll swim to you."

"That won't be necessary," she said. "Just pass me the oar."

Lauriat knew how readily some people could panic, but this one seemed serene enough, so he took the chance. Somehow she got her hands free and grasped the end of the oar, and Lauriat and two other men hauled her in. She thanked them nicely. She was chewing all the time. Indeed, some hours later, when Lauriat helped her off at Queenstown "she was still chewing that piece of gum, and I shouldn't be surprised if she had it yet." He never did learn her name.

Chapter 18

A BIG NIGHT FOR THE UNDERTAKERS

IN THE BEGINNING it had been a noisy crowd, threshing around in the water. Boats crunched and clattered through masses of wreckage. Two or more men, here and there, cursing one another, would struggle for possession of a plank or a keg only large enough to support one of them. Women screamed for help; other women simply lay on their backs chanting, it would seem tirelessly, "Bo-at! ... bo-at!" Many prayed aloud. There were even some who tried to sing, in the hope of keeping up their own or others' spirits.

By the time the rescue vessels arrived all this was changed and the silence of a cemetery hung over the scene. There was not a flapping arm to make a signal, nor did any groan or moan guide the mosquito fleet men to a needy case in the failing daylight.

The survivors were exhausted. They were beyond

117

any further exertion, and did not stir, being in a stupor of weariness. Many were actually unconscious; many more, of course, were dead.

It was always difficult and often impossible, just at first, to determine whether a given pick-up was alive or dead. Usually the eyes were closed, but if they were open they stared at nothing whatever with a fixed glassiness that suggested, almost proclaimed, death. Men or women, they were likely to be naked or nearly so, for they had worked off their clothes in the water. Their limbs were stiff—from the cold, or was it from rigor mortis? Their skin was gelid. They seemed without blood.

There were exceptions. Those who were found floating face down were indubitably dead. Some were in that position because they had no life jackets, others because they had put their life jackets on wrong, so that their heads were held under water. There was no official count of this latter class of cadaver—there was no time for counting—but unofficial estimates had them number somewhat more than 30.

There was an exceptionally large number, too, of dead children. Of about 100 of these, about 35 could be classified as babes in arms, often being that literally; for the ones too small to be fitted into the specially provided children's life jackets had been held to their mothers' bosoms—and died there.

Some "bodies" only learned that they were still alive when other, real corpses were piled on top of them. Miss MacDonald, a passenger from second class, came to consciousness when she heard somebody exclaim, "Oh, the poor girl's dead." The speaker was referring to her.

Even the conscious were so weak and so broken in spirit that they could do nothing for themselves; in most cases they couldn't walk or even stand up straight.

Now and then sailors, with questionable success, would try artificial respiration on some doubtful cases; but they were not, after all, trained for this work, and they had no special lifesaving equipment. For the most part the pick-ups were obliged to wait until Queenstown and the attending physicians were reached. There was so much to be done!

The coming of darkness made the task harder. The survivors, the masses of wreckage, too, no longer were concentrated. They had spread over an area of several square miles; and there might be much more of it, if it could be viewed in daylight. The sailors squinted, straining their eyes. Captain Turner had been picked up because the gilt of his uniform showed through the gathering gloom. The same thing happened in the case of Staff Captain Anderson—or rather, of his body. The near presence of one woman, herself unconscious but alive, was detected when a light reflected off a diamond ring on one of her fingers. But there were many who did not wear diamond rings.

One by one, at last, the vessels, loaded to the gunnels with dead and near dead, turned about and limped back to Queenstown, where, in Frost's words, "Piles of corpses like cordwood began to appear among the paint kegs and coils of rope on the shadowy old wharves."

The proprietor of the largest hotel in town, the Queens, was a German. He took the precaution of locking himself in a closet in the basement, for he sensed, with reason, that he would not be popular with these new guests. The hotel was filled promptly, without his assistance, and so were all the others in Queenstown, while some men, and women, too, were put up in bars, shops, private homes. There was no halt to hospitality.

Many survivors, however, did not even consider sleep, tired though they were. They were seeking out wives, husbands, brothers, sisters, children, praying as they went from place to place peering into the twisted faces of carcass after carcass that they would not find these people in one of the morgues—that somehow, through some miracle, he or she was still alive.

There were three morgues, all large, all temporary—the main one, the Market Hall, being the biggest building in town. There was no question of their closing down for the night. Not only were they filled—there were not tables enough or even benches enough for all the dead, which were laid along the bare floors—but more bodies were being brought in or were floating ashore all the time.

Red-eyed, sobbing, the seekers plodded from one to the other of these morgues, which stank of formaldehyde. They lifted blankets and looked, and shook their heads. They plodded on. They did this all night.

Chapter 19

"YOU CAN SEE SOME COFFINS"

ALL THE NEXT DAY, and indeed for several days thereafter, though at a slackening rate, new bodies were brought in, or floated in of their own accord. These later arrivals often were difficult to identify, in part because they were bloated from long immersion, in part because many, those that floated on their backs, had had their eyes picked out by gulls.

The still hopeful survivors, in any kind of borrowed clothing, went on making their rounds from morgue to morgue, viewing, and wincing at, each new arrival. Whenever an identification was made, J. J. Murphy saw to it that London was immediately notified, and London in its turn sent the word to America. The Cunard offices in Cockspur Street and in lower Broadway had been kept open all night, posting the names as they came, for they were besieged by anxious friends and relations.

The list grew . . . and grew. . . .

If clothing was something of a problem, so was cash. There were those who had influence enough and credit enough to wire to representatives or associates in London, Liverpool, Pittsburgh, New York or Chicago and get funds promptly—the Queenstown postmaster said that his office handled more cablegrams in the two or three days after the sinking of the *Lusitania* than it had handled in the five previous years—but not everybody was so fortunate. Some, to be sure, though not many, had snatched cash before they ran for a lifeboat. One of these was Michael Byrne, the man who had been so careful about keeping his cap. All over Queenstown, grates that ordinarily would have been cold in May were laid with fires for the poor survivors, and Byrne soon found himself before one of these, alone. He had been in the water for two hours.

"I turned my attention to my personal effects and took stock. I first unpinned my little bag and pulled out my bank notes, all soaking wet and stuck together. I went to a fireplace and dried the outside one first and peeled it off and did the same with the others. I took out my little picture with the relic attached to it and kissed it for a quarter of an hour. My next move was for a chew of tobacco, but it was all soaked in salt water."

One hundred twenty-three of the 189 Americans aboard had been killed. Most of those who had survived were among the first to leave Queenstown Saturday afternoon, the day after the sinking. They went by train to Kingstown, where they would take the Irish Sea ferry to Liverpool. A few at the last moment balked at the prospect of even a ferry ride and elected instead to stay in Ireland for a few more days, though far from the charnel-house atmosphere of Queenstown. The others made the trip uneventfully, after dark, at full speed, with all lights out, and at Liverpool they embarked on four trains for London. Walter Hines Page, the United States ambassador to the Court of St. James, met each train at Euston Station, though there was little that he could do except extend sympathy. Page, like everybody else, was stunned. His embassy guest, the mysterious Colonel House, President Wilson's confidant, had predicted when he heard the news that this sinking inevitably meant war between the United States and Germany. He so noted in his diary.

House was in Europe on a mission that was so hush-hush it was known to everyone. He was trying to bring about peace, or at least an agreement to talk. Accompanied by his wife and one secretary, he had sailed on the *Lusitania* two months ago, in March. That had been a turbulent trip, and when the vessel came into the war zone her regular skipper, "Paddy" Dow—Will Turner had been a last-minute substitute, called in because of Dow's sudden illness—had ordered the American flag raised at her masthead. Whom he hoped to fool is not known. Perhaps he was only warning submarine captains that he had American passengers. In any event, the *ruse de guerre,* an old one in naval warfare, brought a yell of rage from the American public as well as a letter of protest from the American government; and the practice had been abruptly discontinued. (When reporters asked Captain Turner just before the last sailing of the *Lusitania* whether he would hoist an American flag he did not even deign to answer.)

An exceedingly soft-spoken man, Colonel House was known to have a great deal of unofficial influence at the White House, and wherever he went he was listened to. He went to London, Paris, Berlin and then to London again. He was getting nowhere, but not until the news of the sinking of the *Lusitania* did he lose faith in his own mission. It was then that he made the momentous decision that war between Germany and the United States was surely coming and the best thing the United States could do was prepare for it.

Of the survivors who remained in Queenstown, some did so because they were still too shocked to move. They were to remain for days and in some cases for weeks in the hospital or in nursing homes. Actual physical injuries were not many and for the most part not serious, but the blow to nerves was shattering. Many people never really did recover, being haunted all their lives by the memory of that terrible afternoon.

As survivors dribbled out, newcomers poured in, so that Queenstown remained overcrowded.

Dr. Antoine de Page came over from the famous La Panne Hospital to identify the body of his wife and to arrange for it to be sent back to her beloved Belgium for burial.

A representative of the Vanderbilt family, a London lawyer, came over to post a reward of £1,000 to anybody who recovered the body of Alfred Gwynne Vanderbilt. (The Cunard Line couldn't match that. They were offering only £1 a body for ordinary bodies.)

And of course there were droves of newspaper correspondents.

These writing men were astonished at the gloom of the scene they came upon. They had expected red rage, ranting. They had seen the wrecked shops of Germans as they came through Liverpool on the way from London—for Liverpool had taken the disaster very hard and had heaved many a brick—and they thought to find the men in Queenstown shaking their fists toward heaven and shouting curses at the Kaiser.

"Instead, we found a dazed throng, docile, stupefied almost, it seemed to me," was the way Frank R. Elser of *The New York Times* put it. "One man, who had lost two of his four children, went around beaming. 'Fifty percent,' he kept repeating. 'That is very good. . . . Some men lost their whole family.'"

This same Elser, a Canadian by birth, had been in Halifax, Nova Scotia, when the bodies from the *Titanic* wreck were brought in, "but as a tragedy that disaster cannot compare with the sinking of the *Lusitania.*" The vital difference, he thought—and many have agreed with him—was that, though the death toll of the earlier wreck was slightly greater (see Appendix A), that one was an act of God, whereas the sinking of the *Lusitania* was an act of man.

The day after the sinking—that is, Saturday, May 8—the coroner at Kinsale convened a jury to consider the case of the five victims whose bodies had been set ashore there. This group heard, among other witnesses, Captain Turner, whose uniform had been put back into fair condition, though he still lacked a hat and couldn't seem to buy one anywhere in Queenstown.

Here was the first official action on the sinking of the *Lusitania*. It was to be by no means the last.

After due deliberation the coroner's jury charged "the officers of the said submarine and the Emperor and Government of Germany under whose orders they acted with wilful and wholesale murder before the tribune of the civilized world." This amazed no one.

There were still those who hoped, if not to see a loved one alive again, at least to find his body. The coast is rugged in that area and there were many small coves and inlets to be searched. The few lumbering, coughing automobiles the town contained were soon hired, and many people set forth in carriages. Webb Ware, the London lawyer for the Vanderbilt interests, chartered a small steam launch and poked into every inlet he could find.

After all, one body, that of a retired captain of the United States Coast and Geodetic Survey, had been found almost 200 miles away, in Galway.

There still remained 140 bodies that had not been

identified. These could not be held much longer. Monday there was a mass funeral, a mass burial.

All that morning and the early part of the afternoon the bodies were being taken to St. Colman's Cathedral, the highest place in town. There were not anywhere near enough hearses, so the countryside roundabout had been scoured for carts and wagons and horses to pull them. A military band played Chopin's "Funeral March," among other appropriate pieces. Flags were at half mast, and a lot of people shuttered their windows as a sign of respect.

Norman Hapgood, covering the event for *Harper's Weekly*, overheard a girl who might have been twelve saying to her kid brother, who might have been four: "Come along now and you can see some coffins."

That boy must have seen plenty of coffins. They were not made of hard, highly polished wood; they were not decorated with all manner of buffed silver and gold handles and knobs; nor were they of the so-called "casket" type that recently had come into fashion in the United States. They were plain, pine workmanlike boxes, each about the size and shape of a squared-off mummy case; and they served their purpose very well.

The day was brilliant with sunshine and the view from the steps of the cathedral, which faced the sea, was breathtaking.

The ceremony was a joint Catholic-Protestant one. This was no time to split theological hairs. Nobody knew, or ever would know, what had been the real faith of those 140 pine-boxed bodies.

In the middle of the afternoon the procession was resumed, wending its way to the Old Church Cemetery, two miles out of town, where soldiers had dug two enormous graves. The service there did not take long, but it was dark before the whole burial job was done.

There were to be funerals in many other parts of the world as well, in many countries, after embalmed cadavers had been sent in all directions. Perhaps the biggest of these was the funeral for Charles Frohman on May 25, a ceremony attended by crowds of theatrical celebrities. This was one of the first of the great so-called "Broadway funerals," though in fact this one was held in Temple Emanu-El, which is on Fifth Avenue.

The body of Alfred Gwynne Vanderbilt was never found. Neither were those of Elbert and Helen Hubbard.

Chapter 20

"TOO PROUD TO FIGHT"

WHEN THE FINAL FIGURES at last were in, it was established that, of the 1,959 people aboard the *Lusitania,* passengers and crew alike, 1,195 had perished. The dead were about 800 men, 300 women and 100 children, 31 of them babies.

Of the crew, 42 percent had been saved; of the passengers, 37.5 percent.

A coroner's jury was summoned in Queenstown, too. It came to the same conclusion as the one in Kinsale had.

But the important full-length official inquiry was conducted by Baron Mersey of Toxieth in London in June. Lord Mersey was the same man who had conducted the official inquiry into the sinking of the *Titanic.* On that occasion he had been sharply critical of the conduct of certain officers. It was not so after the *Lusitania* inquiry. He and his associates

129

held six sessions, some of them secret, and listened to 36 survivors, among whom was Captain Turner. It was not until July 17 that they came up with their formal finding, which was simple:

"The Court, having carefully enquired into the circumstances of the above-mentioned disaster, finds that the loss of the said ship and lives was due to damage caused to the said ship by torpedoes fired by a submarine of German nationality whereby the ship sank.

"In the opinion of the Court the act was done not merely with the intention of sinking the ship, but also with the intention of destroying the lives of the people on board.

"Dated this seventeenth day of July, 1915."

Mersey,
Wreck Commissioner.

"We concur in the above Report,"
F. S. Inglefield
H. J. Hearn
David Davies
John Spedding

Assessors.

The body of the report reviewed again, without bringing out anything new, sundry statistics as to the seaworthiness and lifesaving facilities of the *Lusitania,* the size of the crew, the number of passengers, etc. It brought no charge of laxity or incompetence against the captain and officers, and it went out of its way to praise the behavior of Leslie Morton. It found that the crew had behaved well:

"No doubt there were mishaps in handling the ropes of the boats and in other such matters, but there was, in my opinion, no incompetence and neglect, and I am satisfied that the crew behaved well throughout, and worked with skill and judgment. . . . I find that the conduct of the masters, the officers and the crew was satisfactory. They did their best in difficult and perilous circumstances and their best was good."

The report described the cargo, pointing out that the small arms ammunition was stowed "about fifty yards away from where the torpedoes struck the ship. There was no other explosive on board."

Finally, it denied that the *Lusitania* was armed.

"It has been said by the German Government that the *Lusitania* was equipped with masked guns, that she was supplied with trained gunners, with special ammunition, that she was transporting Canadian troops, and that she was violating the laws of the United States. These statements are untrue; they are nothing but baseless inventions, and they serve only to condemn the persons who make use of them. The steamer carried no masked guns nor trained gunners, or special ammunition, nor was she transporting troops, or violating any laws of the United States."

This masterpiece raised howls of protest from the press on both sides of the sea, and was widely condemned as a whitewash, a clearing of the Cunard Line under cover of patriotism. There were a great many lawsuits anyway, of course. They went on for years and years.

The new young First Lord of the Admiralty, Winston Churchill, had a great deal of explaining to do in the House of Commons. He stuck to his statement that the Navy could not possibly escort all merchant ships within the war area, as that area was defined by the German Admiralty's February 4 proclamation of submarine blockade.

Churchill was under especially heavy opposition fire at just this time because the Gallipoli campaign, for which he had assumed responsibility, was not going well.

The Germans, at first, were jubilant about the *Lusitania* affair, as though they thought that they had done something brilliant. In Munich a hastily contrived commemorative medal was struck, showing passengers buying tickets from a death's head at a Cunard Line office with the slogan, "Business as usual." The other side showed a vessel sinking, its decks crammed with airplanes and cannon, over the slogan, "No contraband goods!" The principal journals rang with praise.

This mood was soon to change, and when Kapitanleutnant Schwieger returned he was not hailed as a hero. The reaction in the United States was sharp—and ominous. American public opinion was emphatic and ugly. Wilhelm II and those around him reflected soberly that perhaps they had gone too far too soon. There was no sign of shame in the German High Command: this was just a matter of policy. Was it worth angering America already? Would it not be better to wait until the Imperial German Navy, which was building U-boats madly, had gotten itself into a position where it could really strike with effect? There was no apology, there was no official retreat, but the bluster, for a little while, was less loud.

In America many flags were half-masted, many store fronts were hung with crape, many newspapers surrounded their *Lusitania* editorials with thick black lines. The cartoonists' attack upon the Kaiser, previously a more or less comic one, grew savage. Pro-Germans no longer dared to open their mouths. The United States was still at peace, but it was working itself into a warlike frame of mind.

Though there had been two whole days and three whole nights to think about the thing, the New York Stock Exchange opened on Monday with such a flurry of selling—Bethlehem Steel dropped from 159 to 140, for instance—that the ticker tape ran 12 minutes late recording the deals. However, this soon straightened itself out, as the bulls and the bears alike decided that war was not just around the corner.

The very day after the sinking, Saturday, May 8, at noon, the American liner *Philadelphia* sailed from New York—and sailed full. There had been six last-minute cancellations, half of them accounted for by the actress Ada Rehan and her two maids, but, on the other hand, nine new passengers signed up on the pier.

The mayor of New York appointed Frank A. Vanderlip chairman of a Committee on the Relief of

Lusitania Sufferers, a body that was to raise $15,000 in a few weeks.

Certain senators sounded off; and Theodore Roosevelt, still in Syracuse, stormed that: "This (the sinking of the *Lusitania*) represents not merely piracy, but piracy on a vaster scale of murder than old-time pirates ever practiced." But this much was to be expected.

On the Monday night, May 10, in Philadelphia, President Wilson told an audience of new citizens that, "There is such a thing as a man being too proud to fight; there is such a thing as a nation being so right that it does not need to convince others by force."

That phrase, "too proud to fight," was to haunt him for the rest of his life, but he stuck to it—as long as he could. As he himself said, the United States needed not only to organize an army but to organize a nation. War was not declared upon the Central Powers until April 2, 1917, almost 23 months after the sinking of the *Lusitania,* but these were all months of preparation.

The thing was inevitable from the moment when Kapitanleutnant Schwieger gave the order to fire that torpedo.

APPENDIX A

THE READER will note that several times in the selections from the Mersey report given in Chapter 20 the word "torpedoes" is used. It was the belief of the members of that court of inquiry, as it was the belief of most of the witnesses they heard, including Captain Turner, that the *Lusitania* was hit by two torpedoes. Virtually all of the newspapers, on both sides of the sea, carried this in their first stories. Many persons perhaps believe it to this day.

That there were two explosions, as related in Chapter 10, there would seem to be no doubt. That they were caused by separate torpedoes we now know to be wrong, because of the U-boat captain's official report, not, of course, available at the time. (Schwieger himself did not survive the war. Two and a half years later his sub, the U-88 then, was sent to the bottom off the coast of Denmark by either a Q-boat or a floating mine, or more likely by a combination of both.)

The second explosion is accounted for in two ways. Either it was the main charge of the torpedo, exploded inside the ship by means of a delayed-action mechanism, which seems unlikely, or it was a boiler exploding or two or more boilers exploding simultaneously.

There were reports at the time—reports firmly believed by some—that as many as seven torpedoes were fired at the *Lusitania* from as many as three submarines. People, understandably, get excited on an occasion like that.

APPENDIX B

THE AUTHOR learned in the course of his preparation of this book that in many otherwise well-informed minds there is a remarkable amount of confusion between the sinking of the *Titanic* and that of the *Lusitania*. To make the matter clear at a glance, the differences are listed in column order below.

TITANIC	*LUSITANIA*
White Star liner	Cunard Line
maiden voyage	almost eight years old
hit an iceberg	torpedoed
2:20 a.m.	2:09 p.m.
April 15, 1912	May 7, 1915
a few miles off Halifax, Nova Scotia	almost 10 miles off Kinsale Old Head, southern Ireland
speed 18 knots	speed 18 knots

took 2¾ hours to go down

went down in 18 minutes

2,224 aboard, passengers and crew

1,959 aboard, passengers and crew

1,513 lost, including John Jacob Astor

1,195 lost, including Charles Frohman and Alfred Gwynne Vanderbilt

the band played "Nearer My God to Thee"

the band didn't play anything

APPENDIX C

WORLD WAR I was to last almost three and a half years after the sinking of the *Lusitania,* and in that time it was obviously unthinkable that there should be any salvage efforts, for the U-boats were active right up to the end. Hence there was never to be any hope of bringing up bodies that might be identified. Since that time divers indeed have reached the wreck (the shadow of which local fishermen say that they can see on clear days at low tide, and the shape of which, in any event, is easily traced by magnetic sound apparatus) but they have not retrieved anything notable; nor is it likely that they ever will.

There was a rumor at the time, which perhaps persists to this day, that the *Lusitania* was carrying in her vaults $2,000,000 in gold bullion—or possibly $3,000,000 or $5,000,000. The meanest hooker that goes to the bottom in dramatic circumstances invariably is reported, afterward, to contain a fortune, usually in gold; and it would be extraordinary if so illustrious a craft as the *Lusitania* should escape this legend. The Cunard Line people have never seen fit either to confirm or deny the rumor; but common sense rejects it, for the British at that time were exporting bullion, not importing it.

BIBLIOGRAPHY

THIS BOOK is a compilation from many sources, all of them carefully checked. I must particularly acknowledge my indebtedness to the 1915 files of *The New York Times*, the New York *World*, the New York *Tribune*, and the London *Times*, and also to articles, too numerous to list here, in the *Review of Reviews, Harper's Weekly, Outlook, Scientific American* and many other periodicals, as well as to the contents of published books, as listed below. The Lauriat, Hoehlings, and Frost items are especially recommended.

I have to thank the librarians—those dedicated souls!—of the Phoebe Griffin Noyes Library, Old Lyme, Connecticut; the Palmer Memorial Library, Connecticut College for Women; the Olin Library, Wesleyan University, and the Yale University Library.

ANDREWS, WAYNE. *The Vanderbilt Legend: The Story of the Vanderbilt Family, 1794-1940*. New York: Harcourt, Brace and Company, 1941.

BECK, JAMES M. *The Case of the Lusitania*. Boston: Citizens League for America and the Allies, 1916.

BERNARD, OLIVER P. *Cock Sparrow*. London: Jonathan Cape, 1936.

COPE, HARLEY F. *Serpent of the Seas: The Submarine*. New York and London: Funk & Wagnalls Company, 1942.

CROSS, WILBUR. *Challengers of the Deep: The Story of Submarines*. New York: William Sloan Associates, 1959.

DOMVILLE-FIFE, CHARLES. *Submarines and Sea Power*. London: G. Bell and Sons, Ltd., 1919.

ELLIS, FREDERICK D. *The Tragedy of the "Lusitania."* Privately printed: New Haven, Connecticut, 1915. Philadelphia: National Publishing Company, 1915.

FROHMAN, DANIEL, see MARCOSSON, ISAAC

FROST, WESLEY. *German Submarine Warfare: A Study of Its Methods and Spirit*. New York: D. Appleton and Company, 1918.

GIBSON, R. H. and PRENDERGAST, MAURICE. *The German Submarine War*. London: Constable and Co., 1931.

HASHAGEN, ERNST. *U-Boats Westward!* London: G. P. Putnam's Sons, 1931.

HENDRICK, BURTON J. *The Life and Letters of Walter H. Page,* 2 volumes. Garden City: Doubleday, Page and Company, 1922.

HISTORICUS, JUNIOR. *The Lusitania Case: Was Bryan's Resignation Justified?* New York: Hugh H. Masterson, 1915.

HOEHLING, A.S. and MARY. *The Last Voyage of the Lusitania*. New York: Henry Holt and Company, 1956.

HOUSE, COLONEL EDWARD M. *The Intimate Papers of Colonel House*, 4 volumes, edited by Charles Seymour. Boston: Houghton, Mifflin Company, 1926.

HURD, ARCHIBALD. *Murder at Sea*. London: T. Fisher Unwin, Ltd., 1916.

JAMES, HENRY J. *German Subs in Yankee Waters, First World War*. New York: Gotham House, 1940.

LANE, ALBERT. *Elbert Hubbard and His Work: A Biography, a Sketch, and a Bibliography*. Worcester, Mass.: The Blanchard Press, 1901.

LAURIAT, CHARLES E., JR. *The Lusitania's Last Voyage*. Boston: Houghton Mifflin Company, 1915.

LORD, WALTER. *A Night to Remember*. New York: Henry Holt and Company, 1955.

MARCOSSON, ISAAC F. and FROHMAN, DANIEL. *Charles Frohman: Manager and Man*. New York: Harper & Brothers, 1916.

MERSEY, LORD. *Shipping Casualties (Loss of Steamship "Lusitania"): Report of a Formal Investigation into the circumstances attending the foundering on 7th May, 1915, of the British Steamship "Lusitania" of Liverpool, after being torpedoed off the Old Head of Kinsale, Ireland*. London: Wyman and Sons, Ltd., 1915.

PAGE, WALTER HINES, see HENDRICK, BURTON J.

POPE, THEODATE. *A Letter.* Privately printed by Montague Press, 1916.

PRENDERGAST, MAURICE, see GIBSON, R. H.

PRINGLE, HENRY F. *Theodore Roosevelt, a Biography.* New York: Harcourt, Brace and Company, 1931.

SEYMOUR, CHARLES, see HOUSE, COLONEL EDWARD M.

SHAY, FELIX. *Elbert Hubbard of East Aurora.* New York: Wm. H. Wise & Co., 1926.

SIMONDS, WILLIAM A. *Henry Ford: His Life—His Work—His Genius.* Indianapolis: The Bobbs-Merrill Company, 1943.

ZIM, HERBERT S. *Submarines: The Story of Undersea Boats.* New York: Harcourt, Brace and Company, 1942.

Milton Keynes UK
Ingram Content Group UK Ltd.
UKHW040713051224
3433UKWH00038B/178

9 781479 430321

A Tragedy That Could Not Happen

. . . an attack that could not be made . . . a ship that would not sink . . . these were all part of the myth surrounding the *Lusitania.*

When she sailed from New York that sunny May, 1915, she was hailed as "the safest ship afloat." The German government warned it would torpedo the vessel but everyone considered their words a joke. The *Lusitania* could outrun any submarine.

But the ship was doomed the moment the U-boat sighted her. She could not run away because some of her boilers were shut down due to wartime shortages, reducing her speed. Over half her crew was new and green, ill equipped to handle any emergency. Many of her experienced men were killed the instant the fateful torpedo struck.

There was no one who knew how to lower her lifeboats. No one who could tell the passengers how to operate their life jackets. No one who'd spent one second trying to prevent this tragedy.

Here, in vivid detail, is the incredible true story of the blundering, the confusion, and the terror of the tragedy that could not happen.

The Day They Sank

The

LUSITANIA

DONALD BARR CHIDSEY

WILDSIDE PRESS